The

Garland

CLASSICS OF
FILM LITERATURE

REPRINTED IN PHOTO-FACSIMILE
IN 32 VOLUMES

Little Stories
from the Screen

William Addison Lathrop

GARLAND PUBLISHING, INC. ● NEW YORK & LONDON ● 1978

Library of Congress Cataloging in Publication Data

Lathrop, William Addison.
    Little stories from the screen.

    (The Garland classics of film literature)
    Reprint of the 1917 ed. published by Britton Pub. Co.,
New York.
    1. Moving-pictures--Plots, themes, etc.   I.   Title.
II.   Series.
PN1997.8.L35   1977   791.43'7   76-52110
ISBN 0-8240-2881-3

Little Stories from the Screen

Lasky

House Peters as "The Cave Man" in "The Heir of the Ages"

Little Stories from the Screen

By

William Addison Lathrop

ILLUSTRATED

New York

Britton Publishing Company

Little Stories from the Screen

CONTENTS

LIST OF ILLUSTRATIONS

FOREWORD

It is well for the reader to understand that the stories in this volume are not offered as literary efforts. They are simply the *synopses* of produced photoplays *in exactly the form in which they were submitted to the studios*. The synopsis differs from the short story in that the former is merely a brief and bare skeleton of the action of the play — as brief and bare as it can be made, while still conveying to the director's mind a perspective of the characters and a ken of the atmosphere. Its sole purpose is to set forth " the meat " of the story, not to charm or instruct. The completed film does that.

The use and value of the synopsis is entirely temporary; once the play is filmed, the mission of the synopsis is fulfilled, and it is discarded. The short story is permanent in character, and usually much of its charm lies in its sparkling or moving dialogue. Ordinarily, all dialogue is omitted from the synopsis unless it is to be used as " cut-ins," or explanatory matter, in printed words on the screen. The synopsis, therefore, lacks the smoothness, the polish, the elaboration, and the rounded completeness of the short story.

These synopses were chosen out of about one hundred and fifty, not because they were necessarily "the best stories," but to show the handling of a wide variety of themes, in a range of from one to five reels, as accepted at various studios. It is with this purpose in view that this volume is offered.

W. A. L.

Little Stories from the Screen

THE VIOLIN OF M'SIEUR

Produced by The Vitagraph Company of America.

Featuring CLARA KIMBALL YOUNG
and ETIENNE GIRARDOT.

Directed by James Young.

When Pere Gerome bent his fine, classic old
face over his violin and played " The Last Rose
of Summer," anybody would stop to listen. And
always, when he played this air, little Yvonne,
his daughter, with the " Flower-face," would
creep up beside him in the firelight and lay her
curly head on Napoleon's shaggy coat, and drink
in the melody as it welled out of the bosom of
the Cremona, as only maidenhood and eighteen
can. Sixty-five years of life — good, pure, sweet
life, — had given Pere Gerome more than most
men get, — the love of his friends, the adoration
of his daughter, and the worship of his dog. If
there had been a valet, Pere would probably have
been a hero to him. The family purse was somewhat slim, but the landlord didn't have to wait

— long; and as the family tastes were simple and inexpensive, the one extravagance was the Cremona, — somebody was always wanting to buy it. Might as well have asked to buy Yvonne, — or Napoleon! Mon Dieu!

The little feet of Yvonne twinkled so fascinatingly when she danced, that many people thought that if she taught them to dance, their feet would look just like her's; and so, there was a dancing class that brought in a little to add to what Pere made with his violin. And big, stupid Pierre, who owned the vineyard next door — he waited patiently for Yvonne to name the day. Funny how fellows like Pierre can always get them like Yvonne! That was the household — love, music, and peace.

But that was 1870, and the War-cloud hovered over France. The War-lord and his Iron Chancellor picked the quarrel; and one day the Prussians came, before any one was aware. They came into Pere Gerome's house, and every one's else; and a big Prussian pushed Pere out of the way and chucked Little Yvonne under the chin, as she stood beside her father. And Pere Gerome drew back his good right hand with the precious Cremona in it, and six hundred dollars worth of violin went into six hundred pieces over Herr Prussian's head, — and Pere Gerome was a prisoner of war.

Vitagraph *From "The Violin of M'sieur"—Featuring Clara Kimball Young and Etienne Girardot*

Yvonne and Pierre went out the back door, and never stopped until they were well on the way to Avignon; where next day, they clasped hands and knelt before old Father Marcet, who had married their fathers and mothers before them. They sent a letter to Neighbor Bourienne, telling him what they had done and where they were going to live; and he was to tell Pere Gerome when he came back; but the years went by and Pere did not come. The long imprisonment and illness in Germany do not form a very pretty story, nor would they add much to this one; except that Pere got another violin from a Prussian with music in his soul; and at last, he returned to France.

When Pere Gerome went through the village street, years after that awful day when the Prussians came to town, he hardly recognized the old place. He found no one whom he knew, and no one could tell him where Little Yvonne was. Few people even remembered him; old Neighbor Bourienne and Neighbor Cailleaux, his life-long friends, were years-since dead. Most of those who had fled that day never came back.

Seventy, penniless, alone. Alone? Not quite. The violin he had picked up in Germany was not like the Cremona that he had shivered over the thick head of Herr Prusse, — but it was a violin, — and Nom de Dieu! who should come out to

him from the house but good old Napoleon —
not the playful, bounding, big-footed puppy, but
a staid and dignified elder. But he knew Pere
Gerome, — trust Napoleon for that, — and when
the old man held up his fine white head and
squared his bent shoulders, and started on a tour
of France, to find his Little Yvonne, Napoleon
fell in behind, as though he had been waiting
all these years for this very thing, as indeed, it
is quite likely he had.

Over the dusty roads, through the pleasant vil-
lages, in the quaint old taverns, always towards
Paris, went the strange pair of vagabonds.
Always, in strange places, the plaintive violin
called people to their windows, and always the
old man eagerly scanned their faces; and always
he turned away in disappointment, and plodded
on, — and Napoleon fell in behind. Hard years
they were for Pere and Napoleon. Somehow the
centimes didn't fall very often; and sometimes
they slept under a hay-stack, and Pere shared
with Napoleon what he had hidden in the pockets
of his faded blue coat when he played at the
taverns.

In Paris, it was, — a by-street, but a clean
little street, out near where it ceases to be Paris,
and you get the scent of the grass and the blos-
soms in the spring. But this was winter — winter in the air and winter in Pere's heart and

Napoleon's. A child came to a window, and Pere paused. The child smiled at him and Pere laid his old, white head against the violin; and as the old familiar melody welled out, a vision came to his closed, tired eyes. He saw again, ever so real, Little Yvonne creep up to his knees in the firelight and listen to the " Last Rose of Summer." And when the last throb had quivered on the still winter air, he opened his eyes, and lo! Yvonne stood behind the little child, and big Pierre was hurrying toward him with open arms.

At last! What a time there was! There simply never was such a reunion — there isn't time or space to tell about it. Only that " Grandpere " sat many times in the firelight, with Napoleon at his feet; and many times the Big and Little Yvonnes came and laid their heads upon Napoleon's shaggy coat, while " Grandpere " played the old song.

JANET OF THE CHORUS

Produced by The Vitagraph Company of America.

Featuring NORMA TALMADGE, S. RANKIN DREW,
and VAN DYKE BROOKE.

Directed by Van Dyke Brooke.

At about eleven A. M., on bright days, a very
small shaft of the sun's light managed to find a
space between the tall buildings that had begun
to encroach upon that part of the town formerly
given over to rooming-houses, and shine into
Barry's eyes as he lay in bed in his little third-
floor-back. This was good enough as an alarm-
clock for Barry — eleven is sufficiently early for
any gentleman to get up.

Too early, on this particular morning; for
when Barry opened his eyes, he couldn't think
of any reason why he should ever get up. The
prospects that the day offered were not particularly alluring, as Barry looked at them. In
the first place, it had been " a rough night along
the coast," — " the coast " adjacent to Broadway and Forty-second Street — and as Barry

From "Janet of the Chorus"—Featuring Norma Talmadge,
S. Rankin Drew, and Van Dyke Brooke

was wont to express it, he had " a taste like a motorman's glove."

He reached for his clothes to ascertain if by chance he had any money left — one advantage of the room was that he could reach anything in it while he still lay in bed — although he was perfectly sure he hadn't. An exhaustive search revealed a latchkey and two cigarettes. They were perfectly good cigarettes, but Barry had grave doubts whether the latchkey was really an asset, the landlady having strongly intimated that it would not be, after that day. He finally arose, and took out the trousers of his " other suit," which were " being pressed " under the mattress, and proceeded with his toilet, whistling. Being broke was neither new nor startling to Barry, and he was not particularly alarmed about it this time; it was unfortunately essential to being a gentleman, according to Barry's code.

As he dressed — you never would have suspected that Barry was broke from his appearance; he was Knoxed, Budded, Belled, and Hannaned — he considered the possible avenues that might lead to his financial — er, ah — retrenchment. There was Uncle John, but Barry discarded him without a second thought. Uncle John had so much money that " he used to go down to Washington every once in a while just to laugh at the mint." But Barry had not been

on Uncle John's visiting list for many, many
moons; nor had Barry felt that there was any
" Welcome " on the mat at Uncle John's " little
flat " (eleven rooms and nine baths fronting on
The Park) for him. In fact, the entente cordiale
(whatever that means) between Uncle John and
Barry had received a severe blow in the solar
plexus on account of certain performances of
Barry, financial and otherwise. And then, too,
getting in to see Uncle John was like getting
into The Chemical Bank at midnight. After you
had passed a searching examination by the cop,
the superintendent, the telephone girl, the
" cullud gem'men " in brass buttons, and the
elevator man, they told you that he wasn't home.
Barry got as far as the " cullud gem'men " in
brass buttons, once, but had to pay quite a fine
in the police court next morning for " licking a
couple of niggers," as Barry expressed it afterwards. So Uncle John was out of the question.

But at that very moment, Uncle John's cun-
ning little fifteen thousand dollar Rolls-Royce
was at the door of the rooming house, and he
was being admitted by the landlady. When the
door opened and Uncle John stepped into
Barry's room, Barry made an instantaneous
resolve to take the pledge — if he were going
to see things like that, he'd better " lay off the
stuff! " But it was no illusion, — Uncle John

had really come to see him! It is highly probable that Uncle John's heart smote him a little
when he saw how his brother's boy was living;
at any rate, it all ended with Uncle John saying
that he was going abroad for a year or so, and
that Barry might as well occupy the eleven-
room-nine-bath thing up by The Park (use of the
" cullud gem'men," et al. included) until he came
back; and that a sufficient monetary allowance
would accompany it to keep it and Barry going
in a manner that would leave nothing to be
desired! *And* the said income would continue to
be paid as long as Barry behaved himself and
didn't get married. The sound of Wedding Bells
always made Uncle John froth at the mouth and
bite pieces out of the furniture; and when he got
calmer, he would go out and foreclose several
mortgages against the property of needy widows.

And so, as Barry settled back into the twelve-
inch upholstery of a six-hundred-dollar chair,
put his feet on a Louis Something table, lit a
cigarette and flicked the ashes onto a Persian
carpet that had once been the pride of Xerxes's
grandfather, he winked at himself in a Period
mirror, and murmured, " Pretty soft for you,
Kid, pretty soft! Hey, you! (to the butler who
had just brought in some wine and was leaving)
Tell J. P. Morgan to come up here. I want a
shine. And tell him to hurry! ''

Every evening at eight-fifteen, and every afternoon at two-fifteen, little Janet Carey tripped lightly onto the stage at the head of " the ponies " of The Burning Shame Burlesquers, and did her little bit, which was good. She was seventeen, but of that dainty, flower-like form and fibre, that indescribable dewy immaturity, that usually is the vested right of children only. Furthermore, Annette Kellermann had nothing on her when it came to outlines; but when Janet put on her baby dress, with the short skirts, the socks, and the slippers, and her hair " done " in schoolgirl fashion, you would have sworn that she wasn't over nine years old.

You would have made a grievous mistake, however. Janet was considerably older than her years — two seasons with a burlesque company will thrust quite a lot of knowledge into the dullest of feminine minds, and Janet's mind was anything but dull. She could hold her own in dressing-room repartee with any peroxide spear-carrier that had been in Al Reeves's first production.

And maybe she couldn't take care of herself! You were never going to " sneak one over the plate " when Janet was at bat; not on Janet, you weren't! She hadn't any more use for a stage-door Johnnie than an Esquimau has for a lawn-mower; and she had a way of making them feel so small that they'd have to stand on a ladder to tie the shoes of decent people. Notwithstanding all Janet's beauty and cleverness, she was still in burlesque — it is said that " without a good press agent, you will never do Big Time above Fourteenth Street," no matter who you are.

So when Barry and a couple of friends " blew into " the theatre one afternoon, not knowing what else to do, there was Janet doing her clever little " Child act." Barry wasn't any fool; he had some experience with the chorus, and he certainly knew how to pick 'em. And the minute he got his lamps on Janet, he could see himself paying installments on furniture and asking the way to the Marriage-License Bureau. He sized her up for the clean little thing she was, and he proceeded accordingly.

Now Barry was one of our best and fastest little workers, and had always been an admirer of Young Lochinvar and his celebrated sudden methods; and it was only a few days before he had Janet sitting beside him in the Rolls-Royce, with $29.85 worth of roses in her lap, and was offering her a plain gold ring and another with a " rock " in it that it hurt her to lift, and was talking very fast. Janet was more particular about the plain ring than she was about the one with the " rock " in it; and after some discus-

sion (Barry was some talker; if Bryan had ever
heard him he would have quit chautauquaing and
gone back to his job), during which she found
that the wedding ring fitted perfectly, she
" signed up " with Barry. Whereupon Barry
told the chauffeur that if he knew of a real reli-
able, Union parson, he was to drive there and
never mind the traffic cops. The chauffeur found
one, and before Janet knew it, she was Mrs.
Barry Burnit — the only thing lacking about the
occasion being, as Violette D'Armond (nee Gil-
hooley, and number two on the left of " the
ponies ") wrote to a friend, " There wasn't no
Bridle March by Lonergan."

Barry and Janet had just got nicely settled in
Uncle John's eleven rooms and nine baths —
Mrs. Jenkins, Uncle John's housekeeper took
Janet to her motherly arms at once, having no
sympathy with Uncle John's ideas about marriage — when the war in Europe blew Uncle
John back in a hurry. He arrived most unexpectedly, and telephoned from Hoboken that he
was back and would be home in half an hour.
They were having quite a party at the time, in
the apartment; the invited guests included most
of The Burning Shame Burlesquers and several
of Barry's Broadway-and-Forty-second-Street
friends, and the place was a bit littered up; and
there, too, was Janet, Barry's *wife!* Outside of

that, everything was all ready for Uncle John's reception. They shooed out the guests and cleaned up the place as well as they could, but what on earth were they going to do with Janet? She solved that question. After much whispering with Mrs. Jenkins, Janet retired, only to appear again in the " kid clothes " she had worn at the show, and with the explanation that " she was the little girl from the apartment upstairs for whom Mrs. Jenkins was caring while her folks were away! "

Anything was better than nothing, but Barry said if Janet could get away with that with an old wisenheimer like Uncle John, she was a pippin.

Uncle John " fell for it," all right, but many unforseen things began to happen. In the first place, Uncle John took a great fancy to " the little girl," and wanted her to " come and sit in his lap," — often. He brought her home a big doll and a nice pair of roller skates the day after he got back; and Janet and Uncle John had a lot of fun, after he had peeled off the Persian rugs. Janet put on the skates and made Uncle John play he was a horse and pull her all over the place by his coattails. Uncle John was game, but finally he got so heated and short of breath, that he suggested that Janet go out and skate on the asphalt with the other kids. Janet balked.

Janet played the piano for Uncle John with one finger, and he liked it. In fact he devoted himself to the "child" so much that Barry got sore.

And another thing — Uncle John insisted that children should keep good hours. At half-past seven he would say, "Little girls ought to be in bed by this time. Come and kiss your old Unky and toddle off to bed." And when Uncle John told you to do anything, it was just as well to do it and not argue, for arguing didn't get you anything. Barry was using a dozen handkerchiefs a day wiping off cold sweat at narrow escapes. Uncle John got sore at Barry because he hung around the house all the time.

"What's the matter with you?" he said. "Why don't you go down to the club or take in a ball game or something. You haven't been out of the house in a week. If it's the inclemency of the currency that's making a regular house cat out of you, I still have a check-book and a little ink in my fountain pen. Go on out, I'm sick of looking at you!"

But Barry was "doing very well where he was, thank you."

Finally Uncle John decided that if the "little girl's" folks didn't come home pretty soon, he was going to adopt the child and take her traveling all over America and such. Barry almost turned a back somersault, and protested feebly.

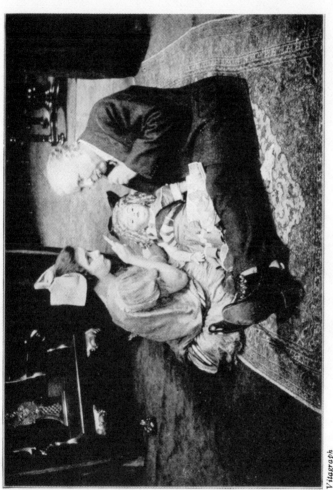

Vitagraph

From "Janet of the Chorus" — Norma Talmadge and Van Dyke Brooke

"Whassa matter with you?" roared Uncle John. "Where do you get off to guide my erring feetprints? I know what I'm doin' alla time! 'S my funeral, ain't it? You won't have to stand trial for kidnappin' if I take her, will you? That child needs education and travel, and she's goin' to get it if it takes the works! Don't never tell me what to do!"

It is highly probable that Uncle John would have done it, too, if something hadn't happened. He went out one day to get a car-load of lollypops and things for Janet. Janet was getting about enough of it, too, by this time. "You know, dear," she said to Barry, "I can't keep this up forever; I haven't been out of the house since he came back. How could I?"

Barry suggested that now would be a good time, and Janet thought so too. She went to her room and in a few moments, came back looking like one of Duff-Gordon's models.

But just then, Uncle John opened the door — he had probably forgotten to kiss her good-bye — and there she was! Barry swallowed hard, and then came across with the truth. Uncle John took Janet over to the window where he could get a good look at her. Then he looked at Barry and Mrs. Jenkins, who were prepared for something like the San Francisco earthquake or Mt. Pelee; in fact they hoped something like that would happen — to save them. But Uncle John looked at Janet again; then he brought her back and put her hand in Barry's.

" You win," he said. " The score now stands eighty-seven to nothing against Uncle John. Let's go over to Sherry's and see if he has anything left over that we can eat and drink! "

THE TREASON OF ANATOLE

Produced by The Universal Company.
Featuring ETIENNE GIRARDOT.

Directed by Lucius Henderson.

When Anatole, old bachelor that he was, used to go up the stairs past the rooms of the von Holm family on his way to his dreary third-floor-back, the prattle of the two little tow-heads, Wilhelm and Greta, and the cheery voice of Freda, their mother, would often come filtering through the door, and he would stop to listen, envying big, good-natured Fritz his happiness, with all his starved soul. And as he turned away and labored up the stairs, he would shake his white head sadly, and think how different it all might have been if only Celeste — but that was years and years ago, and what was the use of thinking about it now! He would sit in pitiful loneliness after the long and weary days spent in fruitless search for work — always with the same result — "Nothing today, M'sieur. Sorry. Perhaps tomorrow " —take his sup of vin ordinaire and his crust, and then he would

take his violin reverently from its case, and
play the rhapsodies that his soul conceived, but
which he could never seem to put on paper.

And as he played, the von Holms below listened to the melody. The two little tow-heads
would creep out of the bedroom and nestle at
their mother's knee, while her hand sought
Fritz's in gentle pressure. " Shoen," she would
whisper. And Fritz would nod his head as he
looked into the fire, clasp her hand a little
tighter, and answer " Shoen." It got to be an
institution with the von Holms, this nocturne of
Anatole's.

But one night, they missed it, though they listened for it; and the next. Anatole had wearily
climbed the stairs after his day of unavailing
search, and there was no vin ordinaire and no
crust. Hunger and disappointment had claimed
their own, and Anatole lay upon his pallet, too
weak even to caress the strings of his beloved
violin. Something must have told Fritz; at any
rate, he went up to see what was the matter with
" the third-floor-back." He knocked and got no
answer. He opened the door, and saw what was
the matter in a second; and in ten seconds more,
he had gathered the pathetic figure into his big,
strong arms, and carried him down to Freda.
" Ach Himmel! " said Fritz, " It is that he is
starving! "

They nursed the old man back to health and strength, though it took a long time and a tremendous lot of care — but what of that to folks like Fritz and Freda and the two little towheads! And from that moment, the fortunes of Anatole were in the ascendant. Fritz knew Old Man Schmidt who ran the big café and rathskeller — "The finest cabaret in town" — and induced him to give Anatole and his violin a chance; and when Anatole had finished the first number, men at the tables paused with steins half lifted to their lips; women were making dabs at their eyes with their handkerchiefs; and even the chef and the helpers in the kitchen had come in to listen. You never heard such a "hand" as they gave Anatole and his violin! And even Old Man Schmidt, case-hardened and practical, and with apparently about as much sentiment in him as a clam, waddled up and shook Anatole's hand — when he could get a chance, for there were many others who wanted to shake it! And the music publishers thought pretty well of that étude — it all came at once!

How happy they were now! Anatole was a member of the family; the two little tow-heads welcomed his return every evening; and late at night, Fritz and Freda held hands in the firelight while he played. Fritz had gone up to Anatole's room and brought down his things.

He balked a moment at the big picture of Napoleon; but he looked at the little, bristling, old Frenchman, and laughed and took it also, and hung it in the front room beside the portrait of the Kaiser; and Anatole always played " Die wacht am Rhein " as soon as he had finished " La Marseillaise! "

And then it happened — *war!* Of course, they both went; Fritz because he was a reservist, and Anatole because his great-grandfather had fought and died under the First Napoleon. They parted with a tight hand-clasp and moist eyes; and Freda and the two little tow-heads wept bitterly for both — for that was their part. The recruiting officer didn't want to take Anatole on account of his fifty years; but Anatole asked that the best swordsman among them take a sword, and that he, Anatole, would show him how old he was — and he did! When the " best swordsman " had had enough, they made no further objection to Anatole's enlistment, and sent him to the front.

In an angle in the wall in the little town, they caught Fritz red-handed — a spy! He was in civilian clothes, and that meant the drum-head court martial, the blank wall, and the firing squad, at sunrise. Anatole stood by, unseen by Fritz, and heard the sentence. And they put

Anatole to guard him through the few remaining hours of the night!

What did he do, you ask? Why what would you do in like case? While he stood guard in the silent watches of the night, there came to him visions of the dreary little third-floor-back; there was no crust and no vin ordinaire, and he had staggered to his bed and fallen upon it, too weak to play his violin; and then big Fritz came and took him into his arms and into his bosom — this same Fritz whom he was now guarding, and was to deliver to the firing squad in the morning! He remembered how the voice of Freda and the prattle of the tow-heads sounded to him in the days of his convalescence, and how they had nursed him back to health; he remembered how Fritz had talked Old Man Schmidt into giving him a chance at the rathskeller. Nom de Dieu! Freda and the two little tow-heads were waiting for Fritz — the same Fritz that he was going to deliver to the firing squad! In two hours the dawn would come over the eastern hills.

What did he do? Why, he opened the door of the guard house, and called out Fritz and told him to go and showed him the way, of course! Fritz wouldn't hear of it, at first; for he knew what it would mean for Anatole; and the old

man had to prod him sharply with his bayonet
two or three times to convince Fritz and to
hasten him on his way. . . .

And when the morning came, it was Anatole
instead of Fritz who stood against the blank wall
and looked down the muzzles of the muskets of
the firing squad. But in his eyes — he wouldn't
let the corporal bandage them — there was no
fear, and there was a smile upon his face. I
have no doubt that he didn't see the grim guns
at all, but way beyond and above them — Fritz
and Freda and the little tow-heads reunited, for
it is given to those about to die to see things
that are beyond our ken.

So Anatole died, a traitor to his country; for
the Law puts loyalty to one's country beyond all
other love. And yet, a very great and good
Man has said, " Greater love hath no man than
this — that he lay down his life for his friend."
And I'm inclined to believe that I'd take my
chance along with Anatole, either in history's
record, or before the Bar of The Almighty.

From "Mother's Roses"—Mary Maurice

MOTHER'S ROSES

Produced by the Vitagraph Company of America.

Featuring MARY MAURICE, DOROTHY KELLEY,
JAMES MORRISON, FRANK CURRIER and ANDERS RANDOLPH.

Directed by Theo. Marston.

For twenty-five years, John Morrison had left
his office in Broad Street every afternoon at
three-thirty, gone to a flower shop, bought a big
bunch of roses, and taken them home to his wife.
He was wealthy and could afford it — but many
who can afford it don't do it. And on this particular day, with the roses, he gave " Mother "
a certificate for five thousand share of Midland
stock, and told her to keep it. It was a little
flyer he had taken, and " while it's not worth so
very much now, it might be valuable some day,"
he said. Mother took it, but much preferred the
roses. The very earliest recollections of Mother
that the two children, Payne and Helen, had,
were associated with roses.

And roses just suited Mother. She was the
black-silk-and-point-lace kind; gentle and watch-

ful; loved her husband and family, and almost
everybody else, too. She fitted into the setting
of Morrison's costly home like a rare old
cameo. Everybody felt her sweet influence.
Somehow every tired head and heart came to
Mother with its troubles, sure of feeling better
afterwards.

Payne was fond of " life "; not really very
fast or bad — just an average young man —
and he certainly loved his mother. Helen was
a beautiful, impressionable girl of twenty, with
all her mother's gentleness, but not her strength
of character. Spencer Delevan, a Wall Street
Money King, widower, and thirty-five, came to
dinner one evening with Mr. Morrison, and saw
Helen. And that was about all anybody had to
do to fall down and worship.

Delevan didn't worship, however, — he coveted.
Payne didn't like Delevan; he knew he was
unscrupulous in business, and he had a vague
consciousness that connected Delevan with some
atrocious act — he couldn't tell what it was.
But Helen didn't feel that way — she surrendered at once, and the affair was on.

John was too busy to think about it at all;
but Mother's unerring instinct told her that he
wouldn't assay up to her standard, even if he
did have twenty millions. But Delevan was
allowed to call, and he was a rapid worker. It

wasn't long before the poor, impressionable girl, in love-sick adoration, was burning a candle in front of his picture on her dresser after the manner of the girls in Scott and Guy de Maupassant and the old romances. And the supposedly well bred Delevan was daily abusing the Morrison hospitality to plan an elopement.

Payne and Helen always went to Mother's room at night for a little talk and a good night kiss. Mother would sit there with her roses and her bible, and somehow, one didn't want to fool Mother much under those circumstances. Payne frequently took his kiss as he was going out, and always Mother put one of her roses in his lapel — a sort of talisman that did good work the night of the studio ball, anyway. The studio affair over, certain highly exhilarated persons proposed to make a night of it, and the girls swarmed around Payne, urging until he was half persuaded to go. One of them tore the rose — Mother's rose — from his button hole and tried to substitute one of her orchids. Payne came to himself instantly, and went home — sober. And when Mother came into his room at two-thirty to see if he were all right, he was glad he did! Score one for Mother's roses!

Passing through the hall next morning, he met the butler with the mail; there was a letter for Helen — it was from Delevan arranging the elopement — but Payne didn't know it — and he took it to her room. There he saw Delevan's picture on her dresser; and picking it up, the feeling again came to him that he had seen Delevan somewhere else than in Wall Street. Searching the crannies of his brain it came to him all at once, passing like a vision through his mind. He had stood on the slippery deck of a sinking liner in mid-ocean and had seen a terror-stricken woman clinging to a man. Another half-crazed woman passed, hugging a life-preserver. And the man — God save the mark — flung the first woman to the deck, and wrenching the life-preserver from the passing woman, strapped it about his own worthless carcass and jumped overboard. Then Payne knew who Delevan was!

The letter did its work and Helen agreed to elope. Delevan's big car was already at the door, and he came up the steps. Then a curious thing happened. She opened the door for him, and he stood there with a rose in his button hole! And as he pressed her to him, he held her face against the rose! That was enough for Helen! All the enormity of her conduct was patent to her weak little soul, and she broke away from his arms; and the elopement was postponed, sine die. Score two!

She reached her room breathless at the nar-

rowness of her escape — nobody had seen her —
and tore off her wraps; she still had on her hat,
when in rushed a white faced maid and babbled
something incoherent about her mother. She
rushed to Mother's room still wearing her hat
and gloves. She met Payne in the hall, he saw
the hat and the gloves, and they told him the
whole story — and he remembered it afterwards.

Payne and Helen had left Mother's side that
night in very tender mood. Helen, with the
guilty knowledge of her impending elopement had
been dissolved in tears. It seemed almost like a
prophecy when Mother said: "I shan't be here
with you very long, children, but I feel that
when I am gone, if you ever need me I shall
come." She kissed them good night, and they
went, leaving her fondling her roses. She put
the certificate of stock in her bible, and laid the
book on the table.

And then she knelt at her chair and lifted her
eyes to God in a prayer for her children; and
as the sweet old lips parted in speech, even as
she knelt, an Angel touched her on the shoulder
and beckoned. The world could ill spare her,
but God wanted her with Him.

Mother's bodily presence had been away from
them almost a year. The light of old John Morrison's mind had gone out with her, and he could
do little but sit in the big library by the vase of

roses, and mumble. Payne had to take command at the office and try to untangle the snarl — and it was a hard job.

Now a hound of the Delevan breed is a hard loser; he is accustomed to getting what he wants. He had always had a sort of hypnotic influence over Helen; and again his car stood near the door and he was in the hall — no rose this time — when she crept down the stairs. As she reached the last step, she felt a strange, unseen influence. Mother stood there, unseen by her or him, but there nevertheless! Both Helen and Delevan could feel a strong and indefinable deterrent force, something akin to the telepathy that reveals an unseen human presence. Mother's spiritual hand stopped Helen and she slowly backed up the stairs. Delevan stood as one transfixed — dazed; and as he recovered himself and turned to the door, it opened, and Payne came in.

Payne had not forgotten the hat and gloves, and here was the scoundrel again! And forthwith, he proceeded to administer to Mr. Delevan a most thorough and artistic thrashing, putting in one or two for the women on the sinking ship, and had the butler throw him down the front steps. He told his father what he had done, and the old gentleman was much perturbed; his glimmering reason remembered Delevan's power.

" He will ruin us! " he said.

" It was worth it! " said Payne.

And that is exactly what Delevan came pretty
near doing. He turned loose all the dogs of
financial war that his vast wealth could muster
against his comparatively puny victim. All the
undermining, treacherous, crooked manoeuvres
which Wall Street knows, and none better than
Delevan, were used, and the crisis soon came.
They pounded the Morrison interests up and
down, Midland in particular, until ruin stared
them in the face. And Payne and his father
went out of the office one afternoon, to get the
roses, as they still did always, knowing that
tomorrow the crash must come.

Among the many playthings with which Delevan amused himself was a very pretty stenog-
rapher in his office. At least, she had been very
pretty, but had grown worried and sad looking
of late. To her pitiful appeals he turned a deaf
ear and a sneering lip, — and offered her money!
The love within her turned to ashes, and she
resolved that he should " pay the price." She
heard a very important conference one day while
Delevan was engaged in the sport of ruining the
Morrisons, and she took it all down very carefully in shorthand for future reference.

And that evening she left her weeping mother
and called at the Morrisons' house. She was

admitted to the library where Payne and his father were holding an autopsy over the family fortunes. She told Payne that the firm had five thousand shares of Midland that had not come to light. " With what I have told you and those five thousand shares you might pull out — for I know something else that I cannot tell you."

At that moment, Delevan and his two attorneys were announced, and Payne hid the girl behind the draperies. Delevan laid down his ruinous terms, and said, " Sign here." There seemed little else to do.

As the old man took the pen in his trembling hand, Payne bent nearer and his face brushed against the roses. Mother stood there! He felt the influence, and stayed the old man's hand and tore up the agreement. Delevan left in a rage, and then Payne went with the girl to the door.

As she left, Payne again felt the strange influence, and it seemed as though Mother beckoned him up the stairs! He followed her to " Mother's room." It was just as she had left it — nothing had ever been touched. He sat in her chair, and thought Mother stood beside him trying to tell him something. Mechanically he took up her bible, and opened it. There were the missing shares!

Hurrying to his father he showed him the certificate, and the old man rose to examine it. As

Vitagraph

Dorothy Kelly and Frank Courier in "Mother's Roses"

he did so, his face came near the roses. It was enough. The coincidence brought back the light of reason and he *remembered!* His mind needed just that to clear it. And just then, the butler brought in a telegram from the head bookkeeper saying that Spencer Delevan had been shot to death on Broadway, ten minutes ago, by a young woman, and that he was on his way with important news.

The House of Morrison still stands; and any afternoon, at three-thirty, if you will stand in Broad Street, you may see " The Old Man " and Payne leave the office, arm in arm, go to the little flower shop, and get Mother's Roses.

CAPTAIN SANTA CLAUS

In Production. Not yet cast.

The country had called its men to arms. Already the khaki-clad columns, in endless formation, marched through the streets, and the artillery wagons clattered after them, in grim and formidable disorderly order. Mothers and wives, sisters and sweethearts clasped men to their bosoms, and little children clung about their knees, wondering what it was all about. Many of the elders couldn't tell either. But Kings and Princes had summoned their armies, and men must fight and bleed and die, and women must wait and weep — for that is the way of the world.

So Fritz — big, strong, dutiful, tender Fritz — took his mother in his arms in the doorway, kissed her withered cheek, squared his shoulders, and marched away with his regiment, to do and to die, if need be, like the rest.

And in the Enemy's country there was great excitement. In the quaint living room of his home, Anton gathered his little family, his wife,

Celeste his daughter, and the two kiddies Louis and Marie, and pointing at the news in the big headlines of the paper, he told them of the cataclysm that was to befall — that is, he told about a tenth of it.

And it was to come with incredible swiftness. Even then, there was panic in the streets. Groups of men talked excitedly — many of them had guns in their hands — and recruiting sergeants were at the doors, calling upon all patriots to come to the colors.

Anton was among the first to go; and he had gone but a little time, when the big siege guns began to boom, and a rain of iron and steel and lead rent and tore and desecrated the temples and the homes of City of Beauty; and before it had ceased, a shell had torn away a part of the quaint room in Anton's home, his wife lay dead among the ruins, and Celeste — little, gentle, flower-faced Celeste — put her arms about small Marie and Louis, as they clung to their dead mother's body, and took on the responsibilities of Mother and Elder Sister to them.

It was to this district of the captured city that Fritz — Captain Fritz, he was now — was assigned. And well he looked after it. It kept him so busy that as he sat at his table at headquarters, he was surprised to see that his calendar bore the date of December 24. Tomorrow

would be Christmas! Little time a soldier has
to think of that!

And yet, as Fritz patrolled the town, he saw
a small squad of his men come upon a partially
demolished top shop — a shell had almost torn
it apart, and the terror-stricken toymaker had
doubtless fled in panic, leaving his stock of toys
to the mercy of the Invader, or of any one who
happened that way. The soldiers, filled with the
spirit of Christmas, and that boyishness that
often takes hold of grown men as a merciful
relaxation from the grim business in hand, seized
upon the toys with the delight of schoolboys, and
bore them off to the barracks for a Christmas
revel.

And Fritz also saw little Celeste struggling
to get a great, unwieldy bundle of wood that she
had gathered into the house, together with a
small evergreen tree that she had hacked down
in the gardens. Enemy or no enemy, Fritz went
gallantly to her assistance; and though his services were not at first accepted with a very good
grace, he carried in the wood and the tree, and
saw the situation in the house. Little Marie and
Louis had been fed from the scanty store, —
Celeste had denied herself that they might feast
— and were engaged in writing notes to Santa
Claus, telling him what to bring, though Celeste

was most dubious as to how he was going to bring anything at all.

The children took to Fritz like ducks to water, as soon as he had smiled away the awe that his presence had inspired; and Celeste was not long in following their lead when she realized that he had come to them solely out of the kindness of his heart, and actuated by the best of motives. He soon had the two kiddies on his knees showing him the letters they had written to Santa Claus asking for a drum and a sword and a gun and some candy.

Marie's letter asked that Santa Claus " bring her Daddy home for Christmas and a dolly with curly hair." The prospects for getting these things didn't seem especially bright, but suddenly, Fritz thought of the demolished toy-shop, that his soldiers had looted, and he smiled at the kiddies and winked at Celeste, and said that perhaps Santa Claus was doing business at the old stand, even in these troublesome times; and he put the letters carefully into his pocket in order to be sure that Santa Claus would get them, Special Delivery. At least, he knew of a big box full of Christmas goodies that had come to him from home — he was sure Santa Claus could bring that — but he said nothing to Celeste about it, only whispering to her that he thought the drum and the gun and the sword and the dolly could be arranged. And as he hurried away, the first snowflakes sifted down upon his broad shoulders — it was going to be a " White Christmas " — and Celeste stood long at the window, looking after him. . . .

The enemy had made a stubborn resistance, and Anton sat in the trench with his comrades, only a few miles from his home, warming his fingers over the tiny fire that safety allowed. What had become of his family since that awful day when he left them? He had no idea, but he told his comrades that he proposed to find out, and that he was going to make his way through the enemy's lines, through the cover of the darkness, and pay them a visit on this Christmas Eve, if it cost him his life. They tried to dissuade him, but Anton was stubborn, and he set out, skulking behind trees and walls, and working his perilous way toward home.

In the barracks, Fritz's soldiers were decking a Christmas tree with the toys that they had " captured " and in the revel were children again. Fritz entered, and they saluted and stood at attention. He told them to go ahead with the fun, and asked if they would give him a few of the toys. This they were only too glad to do, and as Fritz read from the children's letters the things he wanted, the men picked them out; and when the list was completed, they piled more and more upon him, until he had to beg off carrying anything else.

And with his box from home under his arm, he set out toward Celeste and the kiddies. She let him in, but made him leave the toys outside — Santa Claus was going to bring those — and soon Fritz was seated on the hearth, a kiddie on each knee, the firelight on their faces, telling them the wonderful story of how Santa Claus came to be. How, long ago, in the deep blue of the Eastern sky, a single, beautiful star had appeared, and how certain wise men had seen it and knew that God had fulfilled his ancient promise. How they had gathered up their choicest gifts and brought them to the Babe that lay in the manger and laid them at his feet. And how, ever since, Santa Claus, who was himself a very wise man, brought gifts every Christmas morning to good children in remembrance of the Little Babe's Nativity.

And as they talked, Celeste and Marie and small Louis seemed to see the pictures in the embers, and Celeste knew, deep down in her heart, that Fritz was no enemy! They sent the letters up the chimney, though Fritz hesitated about sending the one in which Marie had asked that Santa Claus "bring her Daddy home for Christmas" — Fritz knew it wouldn't be well for Daddy to come — but Marie was insistent, and so he sent that with the rest. Then the Sand Man came, almost before they had hung up the stockings, and Fritz carried them into the nursery and laid them in the crib, and his eyes met Celeste's as they watched them by the light of the candle shaded by Celeste's hand. And all this while, Anton was stealthily working his way through dangers and difficulties, and was drawing steadily nearer to his home.

Then Fritz and Celeste dressed the tree, and put the Christmas box under it — that must not be opened until the morning, Fritz said — and then Fritz looked at his watch and was astonished at the time, and left hurriedly, taking both Celeste's hands in his and kissing them reverently. And when he had gone and the door was barred, she looked at the place where Fritz had kissed and shyly kissed it herself.

There was a hurried knock at the door, and Anton's voice called to her for admittance! In a moment, he was in her arms, and she had told him of her mother's death, and had led him, broken-hearted, to the crib of Louis and Marie. Scarcely were their arms about his neck, when there was another knock at the door, and they all stood aghast. Then Celeste closed the nursery door and went to the outer one. It was

Fritz, who had forgotten his field glasses which he had unslung from his shoulder when he dressed the tree! He apologized for his intrusion and went to the table and picked up the glasses. There was a man's hat on the table and it was wet with snow! He looked into Celeste's eyes, and she dropped them. The soul of Fritz sickened within him.

And behind the nursery door, while the children clung to him, Anton drew his sword and prepared to fight. Fritz started for the closed door and Celeste tried to stop him, but he flung her off. Then the door opened, and Anton, sword in hand, stepped out. Fritz whipped out his sword, but before either could do anything, Louis and Marie had run and jumped upon their father, and Celeste had her arms about his neck!

" You see, Mr. Soldier," piped Marie, " Santa Claus sent Daddy home for Christmas after all! " Fritz lowered his sword and stood shamefaced. Then he went to the table and scribbled on a piece of paper and gave it to Anton. It was a passport through the lines.

Celeste fell upon her knees and kissed Fritz's hand: The two men went out together; and at the parting of the ways — neither had said a word till then — Anton put out his hand. Fritz took it, in the freemasonry of big men — big in

body and big in soul. And as they turned away,
each looked back, and with common impulse said,
" Merry Christmas! "

When morning dawned, Fritz sat at his table
at headquarters, toying with a sprig of holly and
thinking. He remembered how, on a previous
Christmas morning, he had heard a choir boy
with a face like an angel sing, " Peace on Earth,
Good Will toward Men." Fritz's face was very
sober; but gradually, as he thought, he smiled.
War has its compensations.

LILY, OF THE VALLEY

Produced by The Vitagraph Company of America.

Featuring LILLIAN WALKER and
EARLE WILLIAMS

Directed by Wilfrid North.

Old Man Kemble and Old Man Maynard had played cribbage from four to six every afternoon for twenty years in the little back room of " the Dutchman's," on Beaver Street. They had their daily quarrel over their second toddy, and made up over their third. And so, when Old Man Kemble died, he left his all — three thousand dollars — to his daughter, Lillian, who was the god-daughter of his life-long friend and crony. " I don't want any will or any executors or any lawyers bothering around," he contemptuously said to Maynard — who was a lawyer — and so, as a paradox, he entrusted everything to him.

Maynard was one of the old generation; he had a musty, old-fashioned office down among the tangled streets below Wall, where you still

have to climb the stairs, and the offices have
mantels in them, and the janitor takes a fatherly
interest in you, and is willing to wait for the
rent if it isn't convenient on " the first." (There
are really a few of those places left.)

Across the narrow hall from Maynard's office,
Hugh Graham had hung out a brand new shingle,
and put in a desk and a few books, and started
in to take Choate's clients away from him. But
somehow, Choate's clients seemed content with
Choate's advice, notwithstanding Hugh had come
to town; and Hugh sat in his little office and
listened for the footstep of the client that it
seemed would never come. He used to go into
Maynard's office and thrash out questions of
law, sociably and unprofitably, until they became
fast friends.

And Hugh watched his small savings dwindle
until the scoop scraped on the bottom of the
barrel, and he knew that he must replenish the
barrel before he could go on. Now the refuge
of the young lawyer who can't " make it go,"
is to teach school; so when the agency recom-
mended him to the school-board of Spring Valley, at sixty a month and found, he took the job
and took down his shingle — pro tem — and
started for Spring Valley.

Lillian Kemble was, without doubt, the love-
liest thing that ever climbed the rickety stairs

Lillian Walker, Earle Williams, and Mary Anderson in "Lily of the Valley"

to old Mr. Maynard's office to "talk it over." The City of New York is no place for orphaned loveliness sixteen years old. And so it all came about that Lillian should go to the home of Maynard's boyhood friends, Prudence and Samantha, up in Spring Valley, Vermont, until such time as Fate decreed a return. (And having got Lily and Hugh in the same town, the most casual student of the screen knows that something is going to happen.)

"Aunt" Prudence took off Lily's rather modish dress and hat (though Samantha secretly liked them) and they did her hair in the prevailing fashion of Spring Valley's best little hairdressers. And arrayed in the charm of gingham and sunbonnet and pigtails, Lily went off to school. The new pupil in a country school usually creates some commotion — Lily's case was no exception — "only more so." But they all got acquainted in no time, and Jake and Josh began to bring her apples and posies, as is the way of swains in schools since schools began; and Sally and Susan and Sadie worshipped at the shrine of her beauty and her urban ways. And Hugh — well, he just wouldn't let himself think about her at all — at least, no more than he could help; though it was pretty hard when she looked straight into his eyes and smilingly conjugated "amo."

And then the fly got into the ointment; Lily tried to pass a note to Susie, one day, and Hugh told Lily to bring it to him. Now of course, he didn't know that the note said "Isn't our Hughey the sweetest thing? I just love him." But Lily did know it; and she refused to hand it over — ab-so-tive-ly! Discipline must be kept, and so Lily was told to remain after school until she was ready to obey orders. It got late and things were still in statu quo. Jake and Josh, her knights errant, looked in through the window at times, and tried to get up enough courage to go in and rescue the princess from the ogre's castle — or lick the teacher — or something; but Lily finally surrendered, and handing Hugh the note, she burst into tears as she saw him open it; and ran home as fast as her legs could carry her.

The wounded pride of sixteen is unrelenting; no more walks home with Hugh under the elms, no more "botany" in the woods, no more — anything; not even "Goodbye" when the term closed, though she came very near relenting then. But a trustee with chin whiskers was talking to him; and Hugh went back to town with only her memory and the note; and she had only her pride — in which there wasn't a great deal of comfort — and so, she used to cry sometimes into the little, dog-eared Latin grammar where it said " amo, amas, amat."

Somehow, Lily's three thousand dollars got away from Old Man Maynard — he didn't mean to use it — but he did, and he woke up one day to the fact that the box marked " Lillian Kemble " was empty, and he knew that a "show-down " had to come. So he took a stiff drink and sat down and wrote to " Aunt " Prudence and told her the whole thing. Then he called in Hugh, who had got fairly prosperous these last two years, though Choate hadn't yet offered him a partnership to save the remnant of his fast decreasing clientele. He told Hugh that he had spent the money belonging to Lillian, and he guessed the center span of the bridge was about high enough, etc., etc. The old man had become very dear to Hugh, these last years, and Hugh still had memories of a certain little rebellious face in the growing dusk of the school room (he still had the note in his wallet), and of the page of the grammar that had " amo " on it. So, not knowing that the Old Man had written Prudence all about it, he resolved to make good the Old Man's deficit and save his face to his friends and Lily her money. He went out and sold his horse, and mortgaged his books, and borrowed at the bank, and scraped up the three thousand; and

came back to find the Old Man dead in his chair,
with his head bowed over the Penal Code, at the
section defining Larceny! This didn't change
Hugh's purpose any — it strengthened it, if anything; and he set out for Spring Valley " to
render an account of the stewardship of Donald
Maynard, deceased."

When Mr. Maynard's letter came to Prudence,
confessing his defalcation, they held a family
council, and Prudence decided — she always
decided things for them — that Lily and Samantha must go down to New York to see if something couldn't be done. Lily said she didn't
care two snaps for the old money and she wished
that " Uncle Don " could have had more of it
if it would have made him happy. But it was
decreed that she go. She got out the clothes of
yesteryear, and fixed them up and laughed at
them — Samantha was in such a flutter over
going to the City that she couldn't help much.
And just as they were about to start, a bare-
footed boy came tearing up the road with Hugh's
telegram telling them of Mr. Maynard's death,
and that he was on his way to see them, and the
trip was off.

Hugh landed in Spring Valley and walked the
old familiar road, and looked into the window of
the little red school house, and marched up the
hollyhock-lined walk to the front door. Prudence

Lillian Walker and Earle Williams in "Lily of the Valley"

and Samantha admitted him, and he sat down in the best parlor and gravely tried to turn over the three thousand dollars to the two old ladies. Lily crept to the door and heard every word. Now, Prudence and Samantha were no fools; they saw through his generous act at once, — and so did Lily. And the kindly old ladies took out Maynard's letter confessing his peculation. Hugh tried to brazen it out, but it was no use. And then he demanded to see Lily — it belonged to her — or some three thousand dollars did — and Lily tiptoed up stairs as fast as she could go to her room; she dare not face him then, her eyes would have betrayed her secret. She got out the Latin grammar and went down the path to the school house, and sat in her old seat — I think the minx knew he would find her there — I did, and you did — and he did. He took out the little worn note, and turned to " amo " in the book — and further, deponent sayeth not.

OLD GOOD-FOR-NUTHIN'

Produced by The Vitagraph Company of America.

Featuring JAY DWIGGINS, EDWINA ROBBINS,
and BOBBIE CONNELLY.

Directed by George Ridgwell.

" Do I know Mr. Hiram Peabody? You mean
" Old Good-for-Nuthin'! " Sure, I know him—
everybody knows him. Folks always call him
" Old Good-for-Nuthin; " an' I reckon that,
jedged by ordinary standards, that's about his
size. He was always a shif'less, triflin', whittlin',
whistlin', jack-knife-tradin' old party, that
couldn't be relied on for nuthin', at least by
grown-up people, les' 'twas an engagement to
go fishin', or to play the fiddle at a dance or
a corn-huskin'. He never done no huskin', an'
stuck pretty clost to the cider-jug between tunes.
But one thing—nobody ever heared him say a
cross or an unkind word to a child, nor knew
him to do a mean trick to anybody—you got to
hand that to him.

Still, he wa'nt a particle of use to anybody,

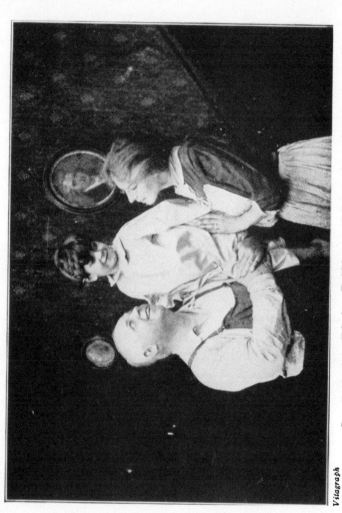

Jay Dwiggins, Edwina Robbins, and Bobby Connelly in
"Old Good-for-Nuthin'"

let alone S'manthy, his sister, that he lived with in a run-down place jes' beyond the fork. No, 't aint run-down now; that's one reason I'm tellin' you about him; tho' if 't had been left to him, I 'spose it 'd look jest the same as it always use' to. Le' me tell you.

Old Hiram wa'nt no account. S'manthy 'd set him choppin' wood or weedin' the garden, an' ten chances to one, some of the kids would come along, and Hiram 'd stop whatever he was doin' an' go off with 'em an' learn 'em to set a figure-4 trap, or find a bee-tree for 'em, and mebbe get all stung up and give the boys the honey, in the end. S'manthy 'd send him to the store, an' there wa'nt no tellin' when he'd come back; or like as not, he'd forget what he was sent to buy — mebbe some sugar or coffee or somethin' — an' he'd come home with some triflin' thing like a string of beads or somethin', that he thought she'd like; an' she'd have to go back an' exchange it — an' Old Perkins, who run the store, wa'nt no great hand to exchange nuthin' he'd done sold.

Certainly was the most onpractical cuss! Leave what he was doin' any time to go an' do somethin' for anyone else — an' him and S'manthy was poor as Job's turkey, too — jest managed to get along. How they contrived to keep the farm away from the mortgagee was a myst'ry.

She was gettin' along to the old-maid stage pretty fast; some said she'd had a feller, but he went West, an' nobody never heard of him again — not for a considerable long spell, they didn't.

'T any rate, right when things was worst with Hiram and S'manthy, — I heared Old Perkins tell him flat that he wouldn't trust him for another cent — heared him with my own ears, I did, — right on his way home, after a callin'-down like that, with nuthin' in his basket, and prob'ly wonderin' what he was goin' to say to S'manthy, what does Hiram do but stop at Mis' Holloway's house, seein' a crowd there. 'T wa'nt Mis' Holloway's house, either, bein' she rented it, or 't least, owed rent for it regular, bein' a widda woman. Seems she up an' died, leavin' a youngster 'bout five years old, an' they was figurin' on sendin' him to the poor farm, him not having no relatives livin'. The Town Commissioner was there, an' the Poor Master, an' it seemed nobody wanted the boy bound out to 'em, being' as the boy would be more bother 'n he was worth.

Well, I swan, if Hiram don't up and say, " I'll take him! " An' they says, " You? " An' Hiram says, " Yes, *me!* " An' they says, " What 'll S'manthy say? " An' Hiram says, bristlin' up, " Never mind what S'manthy 'll say! *You* ain't got to hear it! "

Vitagraph

Jay Dwiggins in "Old Good-for-Nuthin'"

They was some doubtful about givin' the boy to Hiram, him bein' so shif'less; but Hiram was set on it, an' the boy cried and wanted to go with him, so they let him take him, though they couldn't see where the boy was goin' to be a lot better off 'n he was then. Wa'al, if S'manthy put up a holler, nobody ever knowed anything about it, an' the boy stayed there an' seemed to thrive. Him an' Hiram kind o' made a team; you couldn't pry 'em apart no more 'n you could these here — now — Si'mese Twins. When you seen one, you knowed the other was clost by — never went nowhere 'cept together. An' Hiram learned him a lot — I guess pretty much all the boys in town got idees from Hiram, at that — an' they managed to dress him comf'table an' decent, an' kep' him fed up, though the Lord knows how!

An' I swan! Seems if the luck didn't change for Hiram an' S'manthy from the day they took him! It wa'nt a great while before a man come to town lookin' for Mis' Holloway. Seems he was her brother, or somethin', and he was referred to Hiram's. Seems, too, he was the feller that had went West on S'manthy an' hadn't wrote for years, nor nuthin'. An' 't any rate, he got married to S'manthy, an' is said to be pretty tol'able comf'table well off. He fixed the farm up slick, an' has a Ford.

But it never made no change in Old Good-for-Nuthin'. He's jest the same shif'less, triflin', whittlin', whistlin', no-account feller — him an' that boy! Jest nacher'ly no account! An' you say that he's proba'ly heir to a big bunch of coal-lands in Pennsylvany? Wa'al I swan! That's him now! That's Old Go —— that's Mr. Peabody — the fat man with the old straw hat an' one gallus an' a fish-pole. That's Mr. Peabody. An' that's the Holloway boy with him, with a fish-pole. I reckon they're goin' fishin'."

TONY

Produced by The Universal Film Company.

Featuring KING BAGGOT.

Directed by Mr. Lessey.

Tony was broad of shoulder and deep of chest; his eyes were dark and fine, and his hair was black and curly. His heart sang within him all day long, as he swung the heavy pick at " da gooda job " with Mike Flanagan, Contractor. For was he not in America, that Promised Land of Liberty and Plenty, and had he not, by the hardest of hard work, put enough dollars in the bank so that tomorrow he would send for pretty Giulia, his wife, and little Rosa, the four-year-old with a face that might have been painted by a Raphael? Of a truth! And Tony ate his bread and onion with his fellows, in contentment; and showed them the picture of the wife and child that he would send for tomorrow. Even the " boss " looked at the picture, and said, " Good boy, Tony! " And when he got to the bank on that " tomorrow," there was a

notice on the door that didn't mean anything
to Tony — all he could understand was that his
money was gone! And as Tony looked at the
picture of his wife and baby, he could feel the
stilletto in his bosom, and there was murder in
his heart!

Schuyler Armitage, a man of many millions,
drove to the bank in his big car in response to
the frantic appeals of the panic-stricken directors
for his help. This he agreed to give; but as he
fought his way back to his car through the mad-
dened crowd, someone said that Armitage was
responsible for the loss of their money; and in
the blind, unreasoning rage that sweeps through
and obsesses a mob, they tried to " get " him.
And Tony nearly did, but the car outdistanced
him; and he turned away, after shaking his fist
at the receding car, muttering, and fingering the
stilletto in his breast.

Armitage drove into his fine suburban grounds
and Helen, his little five-year-old daughter, rode
up to the car on her pony, attended by a groom.
Armitage lifted her from the pony and kissed
her and they romped together, quite unconscious
of the malevolent gaze of Tony, as he scowled
through the thick hedge, not far away. Armitage was improving his already magnificent
place by the addition of an artificial lake, and
the men were at work on it. He and Helen

watched them for a time, and Tony had no chance to settle his account. Then Armitage and Helen went into the house, but Tony waited.

The contractor decided it was necessary to blast a particularly hard spot and he warned the men back while he adjusted the cartridge and the fuse. He lit the fuse and ran. Tony had great respect for a blast — he knew what it could do — and he drew closer into the hedge. Out of the house came little Helen, romping with a dog, and right toward the deadly blast she ran. Tony saw her, and his blood froze. He thought of little Rosa in far away Italy, and all the malevolence vanished, and horror took its place.

Nearer and nearer the child ran to the almost certain death. Tony darted from his concealment, and almost over the blast, he took her in his arms, and started to run. There was a tremendous explosion, and when the smoke had cleared away a little, there was Helen unconscious on the ground, and Tony was covering her with his protecting body from the rain of missiles and debris that fell upon them. The men rushed to them — Armitage was there almost as soon as anyone — but Tony staggered to his feet with the child in his arms, and would not give her up, but carried her tenderly to the house, and stood by the bedside waiting to see what he could do.

" Get a doctor! " shouted Armitage. The butler and the maids ran to the telephone. The doctor could not leave a patient that he had at his house; he was all dressed for operating. " No, it is impossible," and he hung up the 'phone. Armitage raged. All that Tony could understand was that they wanted a doctor. He slipped out, unhitched a work horse from a team, mounted, and rode away urging the horse. A nurse came to the door of the doctor's house when Tony pounded on it. He wanted the doctor. The doctor could not come. Tony pushed his way in. The nurse told him to get out. Tony would not go, he wanted the doctor. The doctor came out of an inner room, dressed in his operating suit, to see what the fuss was about.

" You doc? " said Tony. " Yes," said the doctor, " Get out of here. I cannot do anything for you now." Tony grabbed the doctor in his powerful arms, and despite the struggles and protests of the man and the efforts of the nurse to prevent, he carried him like a child to the astonished horse, flung him across the animal like a sack of flour, mounted behind him, and rode off like mad. . . .

Helen sat up in bed and assured her father that she was not in the least hurt, and when he had talked with her for a moment, Armitage was

of the same opinion; and indeed, the child,
thanks to Tony, had been only stunned. But
into the bedroom Tony came, carrying the kicking and protesting doctor, and " cashed him in "
at the bedside. Armitage, happy in the knowledge that his child was uninjured, saw the situation and shrieked with laughter; and the doctor
finally saw it that way, too. He examined the
child, however, and said that she was unhurt.

All this time, Tony had been standing by,
swaying a little and getting whiter under the
tan. Little Helen saw him and called attention
to him; but before anyone could reach him, Tony
collapsed and fell to the floor. Here was a real
patient for the doctor! Tony was put into
Helen's bed, and the doctor shook his head
gravely. . . .

In the delirium of the long fever, Tony talked
wildly about the failure of the bank and of
Giulia and little Rosa, waiting in vain for the
money that was to bring them to him. Armitage
spoke to the doctor, and he seemed to approve,
and Armitage hurried out. It wasn't many days
before Armitage met them at the pier and drove
them away in his big car to the house. The doctor, nurse, and Armitage stood at Tony's bedside, the doctor very grave.

" It is his only chance," said he. Armitage
motioned to the nurse, and she admitted Giulia

and little Rosa, well dressed and well cared for, and they stood at Tony's bedside as he tossed from side to side. Then he opened his eyes, and as one who sees a vision, he saw Giulia and Rosa. He blinked dazedly a moment, and then he held out his arms, and Giulia and Rosa knelt by the bed, their heads upon his breast. Doctor, nurse, and Armitage quietly withdrew, and the doctor was smiling.

Tony sat in a big chair on the piazza, weak, but on the way to health. Giulia sat on the arm of the chair, and Armitage stood behind, all watching Helen and the small Rosa playing on the floor. The little girls kissed each other affectionately. Armitage put his hand upon Tony's, and the two hands clasped. Tony should worry!

BLADE O' GRASS

Produced by The Edison Company.

Featuring SHIRLEY MASON, PAT O'MALLEY, CHARLES SUTTON and T. TOMMAMOTO.

Directed by Burton George

John Ward, something over six feet of real man, tethered the little pack mule, lifted his four-year-old daughter Dorothy from its back, unslung his axe, and started to build a home in the far recesses of the Canadian woods. A wealthy and prominent lawyer, he had come home one night from a directors' meeting, to find Dorothy asleep in a big chair by the fire, and a note on the table from his wife in which she said, briefly and coldly, that she had deserted them to go with a man whom he had deemed his friend; that she knew how wrong it all was, and that he had been the best of husbands, but . . . He had arranged his affairs, and taking his books, his daughter, and the mere necessities of life, he treked into the far wilds, resolved to renounce society forever for himself, and to

bring his child up apart from the falsity and
shams of the world, and in ignorance of its
hollowness and deceit.

So she grew up, her only companions her
father, Nature, books, and her dog. He taught
her baby feet to tread, and her baby eyes and
ears to see and hear the wonderful mysteries of
the woods. To her was given — it cannot be
learned or acquired — that almost uncanny
understanding that sometimes exists between the
human and the dumb animal; birds and rabbits
and squirrels knew and loved her instinctively,
and were not afraid to come at her call; and
even the fiercer creatures of the wood turned
aside from her path and left her unmolested.

Under her father's watchful eye, she lived in
The Land of Books. Evenings, as they sat
before the burning logs in the cabin, Ward
turned the pages and read; and in the firelight,
she saw Jack o' the Beanstalk and Little Red
Ridinghood go upon their perilous adventures.
And as she grew older, these tiny but valiant
heroes metamorphosed into Ivanhoe and Laun-
celot and Ulysses, and Jason who sought the
Golden Fleece. She knew King Arthur and
Oliver Cromwell intimately, but couldn't have
told you a thing about Henry Ford or William
Jennings Bryan. She could take off her shoes
and stockings and let down her hair and dance

with all the abandon of a bacchante, but the fox
trot and the lame duck were not in her reper-
toire. And thus she came to maidenhood, free
and ingenuous as the naiads and dryads that
peopled, for her, every stream and forest, and
as ignorant of the ways of men.

And now, too, there was a new note in the
whisper of the wind and the murmur of the
stream; she noticed for the first time that her
legs and knees were bare; and when she looked,
Narcissus like, into the pool, she was more
pleased than ever before at the face that laughed
back at her from the water. For Emerson Peabody Winthrop had come into the wilds with gun
and rod, and she had seen him!

Emerson Peabody Winthrop, of Boston (Back
Bay), and of course, Harvard, didn't look at bit
like his name. It takes quite a man to come
alone into the far Canadian wilderness, and that
is what Emerson had done. He was tall and
strong and young, and the call of the wild
sounded in his ears. Of course, it was inevitable
that they meet, but in the meeting, Winthrop
broke all his Back Bay tradition and bringing-up
into little bits. He peeked from behind a rock
and watched Dorothy as she danced, bare-footed
and bare-legged, in a glade in the woods, with
her dog as her only spectator, as she supposed.
The dog nosed out Winthrop in short order, and

it would be difficult to tell who was the more embarrassed. But there is a sort of freemasonry among those who are "on the level," and they were soon chatting like old friends, although Dorothy had an awful time pulling down her dress over the bare knees. The deer and the rabbits and the squirrels, who were accustomed to come up and get a pat and a lump of sugar, kept their distance now, and looked and chattered their righteous indignation at the intruder. All too soon she heard the horn blow — that was the way that Daddy used to call her — and she danced away through the brush with her dog, looking back.

That evening, as she lay on the floor before the fire, turning the pages of Daddy's Virgil, somehow she couldn't get interested in anything Aeneas did; for his armor kept turning into a khaki hunting suit, and his lofty frown changed into something very like the frank and boyish smile of Emerson Peabody Winthrop. She had told Daddy of the meeting, and he glanced sharply at her, now and then, over his book, noticing her abstraction.

In due time, Winthrop was presented to Daddy, who didn't seem at all delighted; and after he had sent Dorothy into the cabin, he took Winthrop aside and told him that there weren't any mats about the place with "Wel-

Edison

Shirley Mason in "Blade o' Grass"

come " on them, and that he would take it as a
favor if the young man would go away from
there — a long way — and stay away. And Winthrop, like the gentleman he was, after an
unavailing remonstrance, struck his camp and
hit the trail back to Boston town, thinking what
a disagreeable thing an old man like Ward can
be. Dorothy, not knowing of his dismissal,
searched the woods for Winthrop for days, and
refused to be consoled by the deer and rabbits
and squirrels that now came up and tried to be
sociable again. Evenings in the cabin weren't
like they used to be, either; and the old man,
though he tried his best to justify himself, didn't
feel altogether comfortable about it.

" How old is the child, anyway? " he thought.
" Bless my soul, it doesn't seem possible that
she is sixteen! " — but there were the figures —
both the calendar's and Dorothy's! And after
she had crept off to bed, Ward got out a packet
of old faded letters. One of them was from Aunt
Katherine Wentworth, of Boston. It said, among
other things, . . . " and just because you have
seen fit to bury yourself in the woods away from
civilization, there is no reason that your daughter should grow up like a savage, and her life
be deprived of its proper uses and fulfillment,"
. . . and a lot more. The old man sat long
into the night before the fire, smoking and think-

ing hard. And so it turned out that Blade o'
Grass went to Boston, to get civilized in the aristo-
cratic and ultra-exclusive household of Aunt
Katherine Wentworth.

If anybody had the idea that Blade o' Grass
was going to allow the Wentworth home and its
conventional propriety to be a sort of "gilded
cage" for her, that body was mistaken. Dorothy
proceeded to break down, jump over, and go
through the walls of convention as though they
didn't exist. Of course, they were terribly
shocked, and Aunt Katherine's daughter, Katherine Wentworth, 2nd, tilted her aristocratic nose
higher and higher at each successive breach of
the conventions made by "that little savage,"
and even Aunt Katherine, who was more tolerant
than could have been expected, began to realize
that she had considerable of a job on her hands.
Mr. Emerson Peabody Winthrop had been rather
attentive to Katherine, 2nd, during the winter,
and that young lady had marked him for her
own. But the moment that Winthrop set eyes
upon Dorothy again, Katherine, 2nd, fell way
off in the betting and became an "also ran."
All of which did not exactly enhance Dorothy's
popularity in the Wentworth household.

Winthrop met Dorothy and the Wentworths
on the fashionable parade, and Dorothy had a
most forlorn and miserable looking dog in her

arms, whose foot had been wounded, and which
she insisted on taking home for treatment.
Winthrop at once took the muddy dog to his
white-vested bosom and carried it for her, and
they had a great time bandaging its foot, much
to the disgust of Katherine, 2nd. They stood
for romps in the park with a dozen dirty children, wherein Dorothy climbed trees and swung
from limbs to the consternation of policemen,
and against the peace and dignity of the great
Commonwealth of Massachusetts and the ordi-
nance in such case made and provided. It took
quite a little persuasion to rescue her from the
custody of one of these outraged guardians.
They also stood for a most undignified horse-
race between her and Winthrop along the
fashionable bridle-path, leaving the sniffing
Katherine, 2nd to jog along after them in a
most embarrassing loneliness. They even for-
gave a dive, fully dressed, from a motor-boat,
on a bet that she could beat Winthrop swimming
to shore, while the " very best people in Boston " looked through their amazed lorgnettes
and monocles, and said, " My word! "

But when at a most exclusive dance, given by
the Wentworths, Dorothy told the girls she
couldn't dance the modern dances, but could
dance the old Greek ones; and encouraged by
the girls, she went out into the moonlit garden,

and taking off shoes and stockings, and letting down her hair, proceeded to show them that Gertrude Hoffman had nothing on her — that was Dorothy's finish! At first, only the girls were spectators; but many of the young men joined the party, and by the time the two Katherines got there, Blade o' Grass was the whirling center of attraction for most of the people at the party, oblivious to all things but the abandon of the dance.

Suddenly, she became conscious of the men, Aunt Katherine, and all; and the almost fainting Aunt Katherine saw a bare-legged, bare-footed girl, her hair flying in wild disorder, gather up as much of her discarded clothing as she could get in one grab, and dart into the house and up the stairs. She locked herself in her room, refusing to open the door to Aunt Katherine's demands. Very early in the morning, she stole out of the house, and took the first train back to the woods and Daddy.

When Winthrop called, the butler told him that "Miss Ward had gone home, but Miss Katherine was in." Winthrop didn't even hesitate; he ran down the steps and he also took a train for the woods, and succeeded in shortening the journey by various means so that he arrived at the trading post an hour or so after her.

And it was well he did. It was twelve miles

from the post to the Ward cabin, but Dorothy set out bravely to tramp it, accompanied by Gerome, a half-breed Indian, who was going that way. Winthrop followed on a horse. As they went along the 'trail, the fires of lust burned in Gerome's bosom and shone through his eyes. At the foot of the precipice where stood his cabin, the half-breed seized her, and though she put up a hard fight, she was no match for him; and it was only a moment before she was helpless and felt herself borne away in his powerful arms up the trail to the cabin. Once inside, he bound and gagged her and threw her onto the bunk.

But Winthrop was coming fast on the horse, and the trampled ground, the broken brush, and a shred or two of Dorothy's dress that had been torn in the struggle, caught his attention. He dismounted and followed the trail to Gerome's cabin, halooing as he came. The half-breed came from the cabin and met him with stolid, expressionless face. No, he had not seen her and she was not there. Winthrop knew that they had started together, and the man's face belied his words. He strode toward the cabin, and Gerome stopped him. A muffled call from inside settled it, and the fight began. Gerome was much more powerful than Winthrop, but the Saxon had something in his composition that offsets the mere brute strength in other races, and the cause in which he fought gave added strength to Winthrop's arm. Back and forth they wrestled, tottering, at times, almost on the edge of the cliff. Dorothy rolled from the bunk and squirmed her way to the door, and bound and gagged, she watched the fight — for her! John Ward had strayed far from his cabin that day in seach of game, and from the ravine below he looked in amazement at the struggle. Then he saw Dorothy as she struggled to her feet, and he saw the bonds and the gag, and he knew. At the very edge of the cliff, Gerome flung Winthrop back, and poised, for an instant, to leap upon him. In that instant, a bullet from John Ward's rifle tore through his heart, and flinging his hands in the air, the half-breed fell a hundred feet to the rocks below!

" Daddy " sat before his cabin in the declining sun, looking down the path that led to the spring, and grinning. Slowly up the path came Blade o' Grass and Winthrop, the bucket between them, and their heads very close together. Winthrop set down the bucket, and evidently intended to speak to the old man, but made an awful mess of it. Ward looked at them both, and his face broke into a smile; and Blade o' Grass came to him with a rush and buried her blushing face in his breast. " All right," said Ward to the stam-

mering Winthrop, " I know what you're trying
to say, and I'm in favor of it," and he put
Dorothy's hand in Winthrop's. And then, grinning, he said, " And now, suppose you two go
down to the spring and get some water — you
brought the bucket back empty ! "

THE HOUSE CAT

Produced under the title, "Man's Woman."

Produced by The World Film Co.—W. A. Brady.

Featuring ETHEL CLAYTON.

Directed by Travers Vale.

According to generally accepted standards, marriage is the culmination and finality of a woman's life. Once she is married, her individuality is supposed to expire, and even in the eye of the law, she is classed with aliens, idiots, and other incompetents. A husband's relatives, and usually the husband himself, demand that her life be little different from that of a house cat. If she be well dressed, well fed, and well housed, that is enough — " What more does she want? " The idea that she share in her husband's life and pursuits, or that she have anything approximating individuality or independence, is not to be entertained. And many women are satisfied with that sort of existence — a narrow horizon, an ivy-like dependence, and a willingness to conform to what are called conventions. Content, if the saucer of milk be warm and plentiful, the cushion soft, the ribbon pretty and properly adjusted, and if an occasional caress is bestowed.

But Desiré Galloway was not of these. She was eighteen, ambitious, energetic, capable, and a " doer of things." All her life, she had lived alone in the big house with Grandpa Galloway, a rich man, and a student and thinker. He had supervised her education, her reading, and her amusements, and gave her rather a free rein in her conduct of life. The other details of her bringing up had been, and were yet to some extent, attended to by Mary Ellen Ryan.

Mary Ellen was about fifty; of ample proportions, sound common sense, and the courage of her convictions, and had been in the family for thirty years. She had seen " Young Galloway " become " Old Man Galloway; " she had seen Desiré born, and her mother die; and she had lavished upon the child all the tenderness and solicitude of a mother. She loved Desiré better than anything on earth — or in the heavens above or the waters under the earth, for that matter. Mary Ellen's pet aversion was English butlers — (but that isn't confined to Mary Ellen.)

Naturally, under these conditions, Desiré grew to young-womanhood with a mind of her own, self-reliant, and full of initiative. She was given, too, to helping others, and Grandpa's house was frequently visited by those, who, to say the least, were not on the visiting lists of others in the neighborhood. The English butler, Hawkins, was the natural enemy of such; but the belligerent Mary Ellen usually came to the rescue.

"Who are you," she would say to Hawkins, "that ye'd be turnin' these people away? Didn't Miss Desiray give orders that she'd see any wan, day or night?"

Thus was Desiré when she came to the age where men sought her in marriage. The pursuit of her had narrowed down to two; that is, there were two among the multitude who still pursued that seemed to have any chance. James Graham, a brilliant young lawyer-politician, reputed to be high in favor with Mike Carney, the Boss who held the town in the hollow of his hand; and Roger Kendal, also a lawyer, and of wealth and family — accent on the family.

For years Kendal had lived with his two maiden aunts, Lucretia and Harriet, in the old, aristocratic house in Grammercy Square, the dim interior of which, with its stately and severe fittings, fairly breathed exclusiveness and "family." Everything betokened correctness and decorum. Even the old ladies and gentlemen, in point lace and silks, and in high chokers and

broadcloth, that looked grimly from their frames
on the walls, seemed like monitors whose pictured lips would open in protesting speech at
any violation of convention or of family tradition. Here, the fat, fussy, and inconsequential
Lucretia, and the thin and soulful Harriet, aided
and abetted by an excessively English butler,
held sway; and watched over and coddled Roger,
the one man in the family, since his boyhood.
They knew that some day Roger would marry
— he must, of course — and they " hoped the
girl would make him a good wife, *but* . . ."

Both Jimmy Graham and Roger Kendal came
to the party — girls like Desiré must give parties — and this one turned out to be quite an
affair. Desiré superintended the arrangements
herself, even to standing on the top of a step
ladder in an extremely hazardous position, with
Mary Ellen on one side, and Hawkins on the
other, to catch her if she fell, which she did not,
even when she banged her thumb with the ham-
mer. Grandpa Galloway came in to admire the
decorations, and Desiré hustled him out to be
sure that he got dressed in time. Grandpa
started with the intention of getting dressed, but
he was a student, and he stopped, " just a
moment," in the library; and there Desiré, herself half dressed, found him an hour afterward,
deep in some problem. And getting absorbed in

it herself, she helped him with it, forgetful of time, until Hawkins came in and gave them a " beg-pawdoned " warning that it was nearly time for the guests to arrive.

A lot of things happened at the party, not the least of which was the rivalry between Jimmy Graham and Roger Kendal for Desiré's favors. But toward the end, Roger got Desiré into a secluded nook among the plants and with only one interruption, which was when some of Desiré's charity proteges came, he put the question to her squarely.

And dear little Desiré looked at him and said, " My heart tells me to say ' Yes,' Roger, but I have so many things that I want to do in the world — big, useful, helpful things. And are you sure that if we were married I won't have to give up all my plans and ambitions? "

Roger assured her that it would make no difference — and he meant it. And after a moment, she laid her head upon his pearl studs and put her arms about his neck. Part of which action Jimmy Graham saw as he came upon them; but backed out, like a gentleman, before they saw him.

Roger took home the " glad " news to the two aunts, breaking it to them gently — " I'm going to marry Desiré Galloway! " he said. And that night, late, when Desiré and Roger were thinking happy thoughts and building castles for the future, old Grandpa Galloway sat in the big library; but no book was open before him; and when Hawkins came in to ask if he wanted anything, Grandpa didn't hear him, and Hawkins tip-toed out. The two aunts put their arms about each other and wept copiously, and with shaking heads and woeful faces, they " hoped she would make him a good wife — *but* . . ."

It is hard to believe that the three ensuing years could have made the Desiré Galloway of eighteen into the Desiré Kendal of twenty-one. Three years with Roger, immersed in his law — he was now an Assistant under District Attorney James Graham, Mike Carney having " come through " with his promise and got Graham the nomination and election — three years with the aunts and with the pictures — don't forget those awful, spying, sentinel family portraits! — had so wrapped the red tape of convention around Desiré that she felt herself no longer a free agent. And all unconsciously! It all seemed the right thing, too, — impeccable. She had every care and attention possible; no one was in the least unkind to her. She didn't even have to think — they all thought for her — that was the trouble, and she conformed to their schedule. The saucer was warm and full, the cushion was soft, the ribbon was pretty, and she was caressed

— properly and formally. A baby had come to them — she was two years old now — and her name was "Lucretia Harriet!"

"After Roger's two aunts," she explained to Graham, whom she met in the Park one morning; adding, almost apologetically, "Those are old family names among the Kendals." She was having quite a pleasant little chat with Graham, but she suddenly looked at her watch and explained that she would be late for breakfast, and she and the nurse and the baby hurried off. Jimmy Graham looked after her, and his face expressed many things. Jimmy Graham was a hard loser.

The aunts were exchanging glances at her vacant chair when she came in. "I stayed longer in the park than I intended," said Desiré with the air of a culprit. "I hope you didn't wait for me?"

Roger was surrounded by the usual pile of mail and papers, and he seemed worried about something. After regarding him for some time, Desiré ventured to ask him if anything was wrong. "No, dear, just something at the office. Nothing that you would understand at all."

Before Roger left, the baby was brought in for him to kiss, and the aunts gathered round, too, and paid homage to it — Desiré sat at the other end of the table, out of it. When Roger left, Desiré went with him to the door, the nurse taking advantage of this to tell the aunts that "Mrs. Kendal talked so long to Mr. Graham in the park that the baby's breakfast was late."

At the door, Roger kissed his wife dutifully; then turned back and gave her several bills from his wallet. She took them listlessly. When he had gone, she stood looking at them with unseeing eyes and wistful face. Across her vision came a picture of the house cat with its saucer and cushion and ribbon. Then she turned slowly and went up the stairs.

When District Attorney Graham put Roger in charge of the prosecution of the gambling ring, he did it more as a matter of form to satisfy a public demand that many of the pre-election promises be fulfilled. Graham was a close friend of Carney, the Boss, and the Boss had close and profitable affiliation with the gambling ring. And it was intended that the "investigation" take the usual form of a "white-wash," and be a perfunctory and useless thing. And after the "investigation," the chips would rattle merrily again and the Boss would "get his," as per usual.

But Roger went at it with a zeal entirely unexpected, and dug so deep into the matter that`the

gamblers came shrieking to the Boss, and the
Boss went down to see Graham to order " that
damned fool Kendal " to be called off.

The Boss was an icy proposition, incisive as
a razor, with plenty of brains. He did *not* wear
a huge, black moustache, nor yet a high silk hat;
he did *not* talk out of the side of his mouth, or
with a cigar between his teeth. Also, he did not
drink. He was very deliberate, and he looked
like a very successful Captain of Industry —
which, indeed, he was.

After the Boss's visit Graham called in Roger
and suggested that he drop the gambling cases
and take up some murder indictments that ought
to be tried. Nothing doing! — Roger told Graham that to drop the gambling cases would spell
political ruin for them both; that the newspapers
were throwing a lot of limelight on the matter,
and that the office must go on.

Graham knew Roger was right, and he also
knew that if he called him off, Roger would take
his evidence to the Governor and get himself
appointed a Deputy Attorney General to prose-
cute. This would do the Boss no good, and
would hurt the District Attorney's office irrep-
arably. So he told Roger to go ahead; but
thereafter, Roger met many obstacles, which, incidentally, didn't stop him at all. Witnesses and
papers disappeared, but Roger ploughed along,

Ethel Clayton in "Man's Woman"

informing Graham that he was getting to the bottom of things, or rather, to the top — all of which was not especially good news to Graham or the Boss.

In the life of the house cat, one day is just like another. Desiré often sought refuge in the nursery with the baby; but the nurse — one of the " efficiency " kind — was always on the job, and the aunts came in, too. " Desiré, dear, I wouldn't let little Lucretia Harriet have that old towel; there are probably germs on it. And I think that romping excites her too much. She should have her nap now." So Desiré would hand over the baby to the nurse, and follow the aunts down to the library, where, in the presence of the family portraits, Desiré would do a little tatting, for excitement.

Left alone there, her work would fall in her lap, and she would look up into the austere face of Grandmother Kendal on the wall, and assuring herself that she was alone — if one could ever be alone, with those pictures in the room, — she would make a face at Grandma Kendal, and then sit and think. Her reputation for charity had followed her, and people came to the house to see her when in need, and she went to the slums to see them — that is, they did at first. But the aunts suggested that such visits were not only contrary to the code of social ethics of the family, but very probably would be a vehicle for contagion to the baby; and so those things went out of her life.

Once in a while, someone would break through the barrier. Old Man Regan did, one time when his son, Jimmy, got " pinched for somethin' he never done." The butler wouldn't let Mr. Regan and his ragged little grand-daughter in, but Desiré went down the front steps in the rain to see him; and as Roger came along just then, the case was explained to him, and he got young Mr. Jimmy Regan off, after an investigation; for which the Regans were duly grateful.

Incidentally, it was the best day's work Roger ever did. Desiré stole out one day to see how they were getting on, and Old Man Regan produced Jimmy proudly and said he had a good job, " tendin' bar," and that thanks to her, they were " gettin' on fine." Jimmy was bashfully and genuinely " much obliged to meet " her, and two minutes afterwards, he was ready to bow down and worship. The Old Man told Jimmy, after Desiré had left, that if Jimmy ever forgot what Desiré had done for them as a family, and for him in particular, he would " knock his block off." Jimmy didn't forget. Desiré held a regular reception in the street of people that she had known, and finally got back home, with nobody the wiser.

The faithful Mary Ellen Ryan had mourned the departure of Desiré from the Galloway home for three years, permitting herself but one visit, — when the baby was born. She saw Desiré when she came to see Grandpa occasionally, and her keen old eyes told her that all was not right with the girl. And so, one day, Mary Ellen put on her best bib and tucker, bought a woolly dog for the baby, and went to the Kendal house. The excessively English butler opened the door, and looking Mary Ellen over, said, loftily, "All goods delivered in the rear."

If Desiré had not come through the hall just then, there is no telling what might have happened. But Desiré embraced the old soul, and with her arm about her, led her up to the nursery, where they had a play with the baby and a long talk. The aunts came in finally, and greeted Mary Ellen patronizingly.

"I'm comin' to stay as maid to Mis' Desiray, Ma'am," calmly announced Mary Ellen. "Mr. Galloway do be closin' the house while he goes to Florida, an' he'll not be needin' me. I brought her up from a baby, an' I'll be that glad to be servin' her agin." This announcement did not awaken any great enthusiasm in the aunts; but they couldn't really see any way to prevent the arrangement, and were forced to accept it with the best grace possible. And thus came Mary Ellen into the household.

Of course, there was to be a conflict with the nurse — inevitably. Mary Ellen started right in to bring it about. She upset some of the nurse's pet arrangements, and at a mild protest from the nurse, Mary Ellen looked at her — most anyone was apt to feel uncomfortable when Mary Ellen looked at her that way — " Don't be talkin' nonsinse! " said Mary Ellen, with superior wisdom. " I brought up eight children before you were born, an' they're all on the police foorce. Go open that windy, and then bring me the baby's brush an' comb, like a good gurl." For a moment the nurse hesitated, then she opened the window and brought the brush and comb! Desiré looked at Mary Ellen in positive idolatry.

The gambling situation was getting acute. Graham dined one evening at the Kendal's, and little did Roger suspect that the same Graham was to meet Carney and some of the gamblers later for a conference! Graham had been drinking a little before he came, and he drank considerable at the dinner; and he conducted himself in a manner that was, to say the least, a little indiscreet. He directed most of his talk to Desiré, reminding Roger how he used to call her " Desire " in the old days, and telling Roger

that he would never forgive him for cutting him
out. The aunts failed not to notice these things
— even Roger was a little piqued, but he brushed
the feeling aside. It is possible that Desiré per-
mitted the man to be marked in his attentions —
he was her husband's Chief — and she was a
little flattered at the attention of so distinguished
a man. The aunts called Roger's attention to
the matter after dinner, but he laughed at them
and said that " there was nothing in it." He
knew Desiré. Desiré was even then in the nursery with her sleeping baby. Mary Ellen opened
the door softly and looked in pleased at the
sight. The nurse came also and was for going
in and stopping it; but one big, powerful hand
of Mary Ellen closed upon the nurse's arm
and turned her about and headed her down the
hall, and the other shut the door softly. Score
number two for Mary Ellen.

Carney and the gamblers waited the coming of
Graham. At last he came. " I'm taking a big
chance coming here to you, Carney," he said.
" If the newspapers . . ." That was as far
as he got. " I couldn't keep you away from me
before election," said Carney; and that was
about all in that strain. Graham protested his
loyalty, and also his inability to choke off Roger,
saying that they would still be up against the
Governor.

Carney thought a long time, after he had sent the others out of the room and the two men were alone. He looked at Graham in his cold, sneering way, and said, " Well, if you can't do it, there are those that can. From what I hear, you wouldn't shed many tears if something happened to Kendal, would you? "

Graham paused in the act of lighting a cigarette, and the two men looked at each other — it took a little time for Graham to " get " the meaning! . . .

And so it came to pass, that certain interests considered it advisable to consult with Mr. Dopey Louie. Louie was a slender and well groomed East Side young man whose occupation was " sniffing coke " — a " snowbird," in other words — or, in English, he sought solace and surcease of care in inhaling quantities of cocaine from the back of his hand. At other times, he took in a little plain and fancy murdering, as a side line, and could be hired, for a really trifling consideration, to " remove " objectionable persons. Louie frequented the tawdry, red-plush-and-mirrors back room of Slattery's saloon; in fact, Louie made rather an office of the place, and here he transacted his business. Here the emissary of the gamblers came, saw, and engaged him.

Unfortunately for certain people, Slattery's

was the place where Jimmy Regan had " the
good job tendin' bar." At the first interview,
Jimmy Regan caught only a few words of the
interview, and did not pay a great deal of attention to it, supposing it was just a plain, ordinary
murder that was going to be " pulled off." He
caught the words, " Be here Thursday night
. . perfectly safe . . . District Attorney
knows all about it." He thought little of the
matter, but somehow, he kept " Thursday
night " in his mind.

Before Thursday night, however, many things
happened. In fact, that very evening, when the
Steerer was bargaining for Roger's murder,
Roger sat in the library, surrounded by papers
and letters. Before him lay one of the evening
papers; in it were glaring headlines to the effect
that Kendal had the gamblers on the run, that
many indictments were to be found against men
" higher up," and that his own life had been
threatened in anonymous letters. Desiré came
in and stood behind his chair, and seeing that he
was worried, she pleaded with him to share his
troubles with her.

She started to take up the newspaper, and
Roger tried to prevent her; the long strain gave
way, and she burst out passionately, " Roger,
why will you always treat me as though I were
a child, a pet, an incompetent? Why can't I

share your life? Do you think it is enough for me to be well dressed, well fed, and comfortably housed?''

Roger was surprised at the outbreak, and sought to pacify her; he put his hand upon her caressingly; she shook it off roughly. '' Don't pet me! don't stroke me as though I were a cat! O, the monotony of it all.'' Poor Roger didn't know how to do anything but pet her. She took up the paper, though he tried to stop her. Her face filled with horror as she read; she appealed to him to let her help him, protect him, anything; but he assured her that there was nothing to fear. Then he kissed her and turned to his desk. Poor Desiré looked at him in despair; then turned away helplessly, realizing that she had accomplished nothing, and that a house cat is a house cat, after all.

It is probable that to the rum-soaked mind of the District Attorney — Graham was drinking heavily, these days — Roger Kendal appeared as good as out of the way, and that it was only a matter of time when Desiré would be his own. At any rate, he called on Desiré, with a huge box of roses, on Wednesday afternoon, and succeeded in making quite an ass of himself, in spite of all Desiré could do to prevent him; telling her, among other things, that he

W. A. Brady—World   From "Man's Woman"—Featuring Ethel Clayton

had never quite given her up, and that anything in the world he could do for her would be his dearest wish. Desiré did not want actually to break with the man — her husband's chief, remember — and she passed it over as best she could. But the aunts — Oh, they were on the job.

And it was all duly reported to Roger. He sent for Desiré, and she came inquiringly; he indicated the roses, and Desiré admitted that Graham had brought them and admitted some of the nonsense he had said. For the first time in his life, Roger was stern with her; he forbade any further association with Graham, and told her that if he called again, he was not to be admitted. Then he turned on his heel and stalked out. Desiré was very meek and acquiescent. But when Roger had gone, just the faintest smile came into her face as she stood there — anything is better than monotony! . . .

Thursday night came, and with it the final arrangements between Dopey Louie and the Steerer. Dopey Louie had taken just one sniff too many, and because of this, he got it mixed. " No, No! " said the Steerer, impatiently, and unconsciously raising his voice a little — just enough so that Jimmy Regan heard — " Not the District Attorney — Kendal, his assistant! Get that right! " and it was all diagrammed for him again. Louie impatiently and belligerently said he understood, and slouched out, the Steerer remaining.

Kendal! The man who had got him off! The husband of the little lady who had done so much for Grandpop and the kid! Jimmy proceeded to act. His first impulse was to telephone; but that would be suicidal; the telephone was in that room and Louie was not without friends. So he hastily scribbled a note to Mrs. Kendal, in his poor, illiterate way — it was the best thing he could think of — and calling a " bum " outside the door, he sent him post-haste with it to the Kendal home. Roger had missed some papers and had gone down to the office for them; there he searched for a long time but could not find them. The " bum " had his troubles getting to and into the Kendal home — police stop bums who run at night; and butlers close doors in bums' faces — but Jimmy's instructions had been sufficiently impressive about the importance of his mission, and the bum finally got the note into Desiré's hands.

It read, " mrs kendle dopey Louie gang has your husban framed up to croak him tonite districk atterney in with the play act quick "

She asked the bum about it. He knew enough to know nothing, but got a tip and fled. The butler laboriously explained it. Then Desiré

got busy. She called Mary Ellen and showed
her the note, and she sat by Desiré as she telephoned. She couldn't get Roger at the office;
he had just gone. Together they thought. Suddenly Desiré pointed to the words in the note,
" the districk atterney is in with the play."
Desiré determined to get the secret from Graham
at all costs. She called him up — it would never
do to let him know what for — so she asked him
to come to see her. . . . " No, Roger was not
there. . . . Yes, she was alone." Graham took
two or three high ones to celebrate his luck.
This was easy!

While she waited his coming, Dopey Louie
was getting nearer — though she didn't know
about that. Roger was delayed by some friends
who wanted to talk about the gambling situation
while the chauffeur fixed a tire. At last Graham
came. He began his advances as she let him in,
and it required all of Desiré's cleverness to
" stall " him off. Once in the library, she set
him talking. She told him that Roger was home
very little — she had no idea where he was.
Then they laughed. Suffice it to say that she
lured him on with all the charm and witchery of
her being to *talk!* To talk as a boastful man
will talk to the woman he wants to have love him.

Through the French window that opened to
the floor of the little piazza, peered Louie. He

watched them, but he was puzzled — this man didn't act like Louie's idea of a husband! Desiré had the astonished butler bring in champagne, and she plied Graham with it. Graham was talking now — he was sure of her. She had come to sit beside him upon the divan and he attempted to take her into his arms.

" But my husband! " she murmured. " If he were . . . "

Graham rose and gulped down a goblet of wine. Then coming close to her, he said, " He needn't bother you! Before morning he will be out of the way! "

Desiré controlled herself with an effort. So Graham *was* in the plot! She rose and paced the room as though to compose herself. As she paced, she saw the evil face of Louie at the window out of the corner of her eye. She did not start, but she did some quick thinking. Louie softly opened the window a trifle, so that he could hear and determine if this was the man.

Desiré walked back to Graham, and deliberately, almost playfully, said, " Why, Roger Kendal! my dear husband, you have been drinking too much! "

Her eyes unconsciously sought the window, and Graham, puzzled at her words, looked too, but just a trifle late! Dopey Louie had heard the words, and he fired. And as he turned to

flee, that was the last minute of personal liberty
he ever had. The bulky form of Mary Ellen
Ryan fell upon him, and she pinned the slender
little scorpion to the floor of the piazza, wrenched
the revolver from his hand, and applied the butt
of it to his bullet head, until Dopey Louie lay
still.

In the library, Graham staggered and fell;
but his closing eyes had seen enough to let him
know that he had been duped and fooled; and
if that was any satisfaction to him, he was welcome to it.

Mary Ellen had come round the house to hear
the talk between Desiré and Graham, and had
spotted Louie on the little piazza, shortly before
he shot, and she concluded it was best to attend
to him. Of course, there was great confusion in
the house; everybody burst into the library, and
then the butler went out and brought in the
police. Mary Ellen dragged in the pulverized
Louie; and maybe the aunts weren't right there
in " the disgraceful scene! "

In the midst of it all, Roger walked in. There
was the wreck of the wine-cooler and the glasses,
and there was the dead body of Graham. The
police took Louie, who had partially " come to,"
and Mary Ellen to the station house; and Roger,
of course, went with them. Deaf to her half
incoherent explanations, he paused long enough

to tell Desiré that she had disgraced him, his name, his home, and his child, and that this was the end. He wouldn't listen to anything. At the mention of the baby, the two aunts slipped out, took the baby from the nursery, and went with it to their room and barricaded the door.

Desiré at last staggered out and went to the nursery — the baby was gone. She went to the aunts' room, and was denied entrance, while they told her through the door what a wicked woman she was. And at last, Desiré crept down the stairs and out the door, finally knocking at the door of Grandpa's home, where she was admitted by the wondering Hawkins, who kindled a fire for her in the old drawing room. There she sat, her head in her hands, looking into the blaze.

At the police station, after the usual preliminaries, the battered Louie was locked up, and Mary Ellen said to Roger that they must get back to Desiré.

" Mrs. Kendal! " said Roger, scornfully. " After this disgraceful night, there is no Mrs. Kendal. She can go to her grandfather, or to the devil, I don't care which! "

Then a great light broke over Mary Ellen Ryan. She put one powerful hand upon his shoulder, and with the other she produced Jimmy Regan's note, which she had put into her bosom at the telephone. " Are ye blind, man, that ye don't see the good wife ye have? Can't ye see that she lured the dead man who knew all about it, and gave him drink to loosen his tongue that she might give ye warnin'? Didn't she tell me the plan before she done it?"

Roger began to see a great light!

But Mary was pitiless — " Don't ye understand that it was *you* the murtherin' little Wop was tryin' to kill, an' that he thought he was her husband?" Roger took Mary Ellen into a cab, on the run, and hurried for home.

The two aunts heard the car, and ran downstairs, leaving their door open. " She's gone," they said, " but we have the baby safe." And they half dragged Roger into the library from which the body had been removed. Mary Ellen lumbered up the stairs as fast as her bulk would permit.

And while Roger, who had had time to think things over, was telling his astonished aunts that they didn't understand at all, and that he was going to beg Desiré on bended knee to come back to him, and that when she came, it would be just as well if they were not there — they were independent and could live anywhere — Mary Ellen, the baby in her arms, was well on her way to Desiré in the old Galloway home.

Roger, when he got through with the aunts,

called up the Galloway house, and the butler answered. " Yes, sir, Mrs. Kendal is here. she says that she doesn't wish to speak with you, sir. Sorry, sir. Yes, sir." Roger lost little time in getting there. Mary Ellen had come with the baby, and they made a pretty group about the fire when he stepped into the room, with all the humility that a gentleman feels when he has wronged a woman.

There isn't any more to tell; except that Mary Ellen put Desiré and the baby into Roger's arms, and waddled clumsily out and closed the door softly behind her, making little dabs at her kind old eyes with the corner of her apron.

A CALIPH OF THE NEW BAGDAD

Produced by The Vitagraph Company of America.

Featuring LEAH BAIRD and VAN DYKE BROOKE.

Directed by Van Dyke Brooke.

Very few people would have guessed that, twenty-five years before, Van Dyke Brown had been an actor — a " regular " one — who played leads, did black-face, shifted scenes, and doubled in the orchestra and box-office. He was now nearly fifty, was five or ten times a millionaire, and a power in " The Street." Erect, energetic, commanding, he dominated any situation in which he found himself. He was clothed, haber-dashed, shod, shined, manicured, and polished up to the last notch; and his address was Fifth Avenue, Wall Street, Newport, Palm Beach, London, Paris, and Monte Carlo.

When he drove home from a Board meeting one day, after whipping into line a few recalci-trants who opposed his policies, his big twin-six hit Higgins — age fifty, who played juvenile leads, when he got the chance — and knocked him into a heap almost at the door of Van Dyke's Fifth Avenue palace. The chauffeur and Van Dyke picked up the resilient and unhurt Higgins, brushed him off, thrust a roll of bills into his willing hand, took his name and address, and Van Dyke insisted that he go home in the car.

Higgins lolled back on the twelve-inch upholstery, his hat on the back of his head, a big cigar in his mouth, and grandiloquently offered a tip to the smiling chauffeur when the car landed him at the little, run-down rooming house in West Fourteenth Street. He told the other roomers all about it six times; and La Petite, who " done a refined dancing act," said that he was " one lucky guy."

And that evening, Van Dyke sat at dinner in his dining room with the " hundred-thousand-dollar ceiling," as the newspapers called it, took out the paper with the address on it — " 345 W. 14th Street," it read — and elusive Memory played her tricks upon him. He couldn't quite figure what there was familiar about it.

Mrs. Brown and her daughter went to the opera that night, and were to sail for Europe in the morning, and Van Dyke sat in his big library thinking. He went to the panel safe and took out an old lock-box that he hadn't opened in years. There were the old play-bills and programmes; and as he looked them over, he laughed at the times that he and Canby had had together when they played the one-night stands in the Corn Belt. And down in the bottom of the box was a packet of faded letters addressed to "Mr. Van Brown, No. 345 West 14th St.!"

It all came back with a rush. Alice Wynne — but he put the letters quickly back into the box and locked it, squared his shoulders, and took to pacing the room. Mrs. Brown and Emily came it at twelve-thirty, and he was still pacing. He kissed them affectionately, and gave them a cheque that made them whistle at his generosity, and kiss him again. He saw them off on the steamer next morning; and on his way back, he told the chauffeur to drive through West Fourteenth Street. They passed "345." There is was — not changed a particle! And as he sat in the library, he said to himself, "Why not? What is to prevent me spending a few days at '345'? Maybe some of the old gang are there." He made up his mind quickly and went, taking the lock-box.

In half an hour, he was down at "Louis'," and had arrayed himself in some "actor clothes," had bought a few costumes for the old parts, and a banjo — he hadn't touched one in years. His white, patrician beard, the pride of

Tony's art and heart — he had hesitated about that; but off it came! And Van Dyke Brown, millionaire, clubman, and man of affairs, dickered with the little old landlady for the little, old, dingy "third-floor-back" at "345"! He got it.

It was the same room, same paper, same everything. There on the closet door, he found his own initials linked with those of Alice Wynne, "1890"! The people, too, seemed just about the same — friendly and hospitable as ever. And that evening, when Mrs. Brown and Emily sat on deck in the steamer chairs, with visions of "Poor, dear, lonesome Papa" sitting alone in the big library, Van Dyke sat with the player folk on the front steps of "345," and chipped in with the others so that Barrett, "the Heavy," might take the big pitcher, and go over to "the Dutchman's!"

Of course, he met Canby — the story wouldn't be any good unless he did. Canby, still on the stage, always came back to "345." It was "home" to him now, and it had many advantages — you could always "hang up" the Little Old Landlady, and that was convenient for Canby, at times. What a time he and Canby had as they talked over old days, and acted the old parts! Uncle Tom and Legree, and the endmen, Tambo and Bones, and the Statue clog with the whirlwind finish, their arms on each other's shoulders, and all the rest of it. The roomers made Van Dyke's room their " hang-out;" Barrett and Mrs. Forrest, and Higgins, resplendent in his new raiment, the product of his " accident," and who didn't recognize Van Dyke, sans beard; and Alice Lake and Jim McCarthy, who were always bracketed. For it was no secret that as soon as Jim " made the riffle," he and Alice were going to take a chance in The Little Church Around the Corner.

And when the big " growler " was full and the delicatessen was on the table, Barrett, the " Heavy," would examine his shoes, to which there were no soles (he wore a pair of rubbers that Canby gave him, all through the hot weather) and tell, gravely, how, " Belasco says to me, ' Barry, Old Pal, you simply gotta go with me next season.' And I says, ' Not for no two hundred a week, Dave,' I says." And Mrs. Forrest, with a toothbrush-mug full of beer in one hand, and a pig's foot in the other, would say, " This Bernhardt woman is punk. Why, once in Peoria . . . " but the offer of another pig's foot usually prevented anybody knowing what happened in Peoria. And La Petite " could have went with Gertrude Hoffman last season, only she was scared I would take it all away from her." They hadn't changed a bit!

One morning, Van Dyke and Canby started out to see the booking agents. Rosenbaum, Inc., kept them waiting over an hour and Van Dyke got hot under the collar — he wasn't used to waiting. And when Rosenbaum came out of his office with a fat friend, he treated them like cattle. Van Dyke forgot himself long enough to say, " You insufferable hound, I own this building, and I'll put you out of it tomorrow! " And Rosenbaum, Inc., and his fat friend laughed long and loud and tapped their foreheads as Van Dyke and Canby were hustled out.

As they passed down Fifth Avenue, Van Dyke absent-mindedly stepped up the steps of his own house, and Canby really did think he was crazy. " What's the matter with you today; do you think you own that building too? " Van Dyke tried to laugh it off, but at the next corner Canby left him, with some apprehension in his manner.

Alice, feeling sorry for him, slipped him half a dollar, when he came to the steps, rather tired, and said he was hungry. Van Dyke took it and put it in an inner compartment of his wallet, for he wanted to keep it, and as he had just changed a thousand dollar bill, he had some change in his pocket and it might get mixed!

Van had grown very fond of Alice Lake. The very first day that he came to " 345," as he was getting settled in his room, he heard her singing at the piano in her room on the floor below. Van listened as long as she sang; and after a while, he asked that he might come in and listen. On the table in Alice's room was a picture; Van started when he saw it, and sat looking at it for a long time. " That is my mother's picture," she said. " Her stage name was Alice Wynne, and she used to live in this very room ever so many years ago! " Well Van knew it! And after the songs were over, he went back to his room and was tempted to get out the old letters addressed to " Van Brown, 345 W. 14th St.," though finally he shook his head; but he did go to the door and look again at the initials — VBAW — enclosed in a heart. He thought he might conscientiously pay that much homage to auld lang syne.

It was a great day for those at " 345 " when Van decided to pay them a visit. Came a time when the landlord wouldn't wait any longer for the rent, and the tearful, little old lady held a conference with the roomers in Alice Lake's room — a sort of family conference — she had to have seventy-five dollars next day! Van heard the " bad news " from the hall above.

He wasn't taken into the conference; in the first place, he was a new member, and after hearing Canby tell of the occurrence at Rosenbaum's and on The Avenue, they figured he was " a little off."

" Yes, sir," said Canby, " you oughta seen him! He swelled up like a poisoned pup at Rosenbaum, an' he says, ' I own this buildin' an' I'll have you thrown out!' he says; an' I gets him out as quick as I can. An' comin' down The Avenue, he lopes right into a million dollar dump, about the size of The Waldorf, that mebbe belongs to Ping Pong Morgan or Abraham Carnegie, or one o' them kind o' people. An' I says, ' Say, do you think you own that buildin', too?' I says; an' at the next corner, I blows, not wantin' no ride in the hurry-up wagon. Wheels in his bean, sure! An' he's a right guy, too. I wisht he *did* have money!" Barrett reached out and picked up the can and finished it contemplatively, much to the indignation of La Petite, who was about to reach for it also.

" ' Right guy ' is right," she said, looking meaningly at Barrett. " There's a lot of gazooks in this camp that could be learnt manners by him! Where do you get off to inhale all them suds, anyway? I was invited here to breakfast, not you!"

The conference was futile — nobody had a cent. It was suggested that a fund could be raised if Higgins would pawn his new " scenery;" but this proposition was not acceptable to Higgins.

La Petite was disgusted. " Say! " she said, with fine scorn, " don't youse hams know that if Mis' Lucretia ain't there with that piece o' change by tomorrow, you all ain't got no more home than a rabbit? You big four-flushes better quit stallin' and get busy! Go out an' break a jewelry window, or somethin'. It's comin' to her an' we gotta get it! I'm goin' out an' dig — somehow! "

That evening, the little landlady got a special delivery, and in it was a receipt for the arrears and six months in advance. No one knew anything about it, and the landlord refused to talk of it at all — " It's paid, ain't it? Well —— "

" Say! " said La Petite, looking at Barrett pityingly. " You're the wise fish that don't fall for that miracle stuff, hey? Never nuthin' happened like when them cravens handed out manna to this here — now — Whoozis, when he was gonna croak from starvin' in the woods, or someplace? Back up! Nuthin' but a miracle could pull off a stunt like this in New York, an' on Fourteenth Street, too! Me for Billy Sunday, after this! "

Mr. Archibald Rivers, millionaire, clubman, etc., etc., came to Rosenbaum, Inc., to secure talent for his wife's musicale. Alice Lake was just leaving, disappointed. Rivers got one good peek at her, and had Rosenbaum call her back —

Rivers was some little " chooser " himself. He had Rosenbaum engage her to sing at the musicale, and insisted that she get fifty dollars; as Rosenbaum got a percentage, he was willing to have her get a thousand.

Then Rivers put up a job with Rosenbaum, Inc. — " I want to string this chicken along and make her think I'm going to back her in a musical comedy — you know, the old stuff. You feed that to her, and I'll see that you get yours."

So Rosenbaum " fed " her " that stuff," and Alice was in the seventh heaven. Jimmy Mc-Carthy was correspondingly depressed. Thus it became necessary that Rivers called frequently at " 345 " to see Alice about arrangements. " As soon as Mr. Rosenbaum finds a suitable play —— "

Van saw Rivers one evening as he passed through the hall, and knew him for the scoundrel he was. Rivers had just invited Alice " to come up to Victor's to get a bite of something, and see Mr. Rosenbaum, who might be there." Van stepped to the telephone in the hall, and called up the number of Rivers's house. Hearing the number, Rivers came into the hall, and did not recognize Van.

" That's my house you're calling," said Rivers.

" Yes," said Van, " I thought your wife might

like to make the game at Victor's three-handed."
Rivers took another look at Van, and putting on
his hat and coat, went away from there.

It is highly probable that Jimmy McCarthy
consoled Alice for the loss of her " chance " in
musical comedy, for the next day they told Van
that they had concluded not to wait any longer
in the matter of The Little Church Around the
Corner. Van was glad to hear it, and he gave
Alice a cheque for a thousand dollars to start
the flat with. Then he gave her a fatherly kiss,
and said he would arrange a little supper for
them in his rooms that evening, and went up the
stairs. Jimmy took the cheque from Alice gently,
and shook his head sadly, as he tore it in pieces.
" Poor, kindly old chap! He thinks he's rich! "
And he threw the pieces into the wastebasket.

Van got all the others together and invited
them to the supper — " he thought he knew of
a confiding little restaurant that he could ' hang
up;' " and after he had gone, Barrett and Canby
tapped their foreheads and said, " To bad! Too
bad! " And when the little landlady got a
message from Van, saying that " it would be
impossible for him to be at the dinner and hoped
they'd excuse him and enjoy themselves," they
laughed all the harder, and said, " I told you so!
Nobody home! "

But even at that moment, the decorator and

the florist and the cooks and the waiters and the champagne and the rest of the things began to arrive, and the " knockers " couldn't account for it at all. Van had gone to Sherry's and told an obsequious manager " to go as far as he liked," and send the bill to him.

What a feast they had! Van's old room was transformed. When the bride and groom came, they toasted them, and they toasted themselves, and their Art, and many other things that needed it. Finally La Petite suggested that they hadn't toasted Van. They did it — twice. " Say! " said La Petite, looking witheringly at Barrett, who was using a nut-cracker to open a stuffed olive, " I guess you wisenheimers had this bird's number — *not!* You couldn't pick a live one in Pittsburgh! If this here Van is crazy in the head, I'm sorry I'm sane! An' if you simps think he don't own that shack on The Avenue, you can win a bet from me. Why, a blind man can see that he's the goods! I guess this little repast come from Child's, hey? If he ain't a honest-to-Gawd millionaire, then I'm Hetty Green. An' I guess now it ain't so much to the Sherlock Holmes who come across with the money for the rent that time! "

A great light was beginning to break over Jimmy McCarthy. He tore madly out of the

room and pawed over the contents of a wastebasket frantically. When he got the pieces of
the cheque pasted together, he showed it to them.
Then they toasted Van again.

And at that particular moment, Van was
standing at the rail of an out-going liner, holding
a worn half-dollar in his hand. And as he
looked at the fast receding sky-line of The Big
Town, he smiled.

FLEUR DE LYS

Produced under title,
"Celeste, of The Ambulance Corps."

Produced by The Edison Company.

Featuring SHIRLEY MASON.

Directed by Burton George.

It was ten o'clock when Celeste opened her
eyes and looked around the luxurious room.
Yes, it wasn't a dream — there were the flowers
and the other things that proved it, and she
closed her eyes again to review the events of
the coming-out party of the night before — the
dances and the men and the gaiety of it all.
The maid came in and pulled aside the heavy
hangings from the windows: Isabel and Estelle
and Fanchette burst in and sat, as the maid
combed her hair, telling her how jolly the affair
had been, and the million other things that girls
talk about after a party.

Then there was breakfast with Grandpere.
She took his newspapers away from him and

Shirley Mason and Charles Sutton in "Celeste of the Ambulance Corps"

dragged him out of his chair to make him dance with her, until he surrendered unconditionally and begged for mercy.

Then there was the ride to the matinee in the big car; Harold and Percy and Reggie met them and rode home in the car with her, which was held up by a lot of people who were watching a bulletin-board with "WAR" in big letters upon it.

"Deuced bore, this war business," said Harold. "You girls cawn't get your Paris gowns this season, y' know."

She found Grandpere in the big library, very solemn over his newspaper — Grandpere had been through the war of '70, and knew. She took his cane and played soldier before him — but he wasn't to be amused. And she, who had always lived in the Land of Never-a-Care, couldn't understand it, quite.

Then three of Grandpere's old friends came in for dinner, and they were very troubled, too — one of them had but one arm, the other he had left somewhere near Metz, in '70. And another had sightless eyes — from a shell explosion in the same war. They sat at dinner, and the four grizzled veterans told of that awful year — '70, while she listened with widening eyes. Grandpere told how he lay upon the field and of how a woman, a nurse, had come and ministered to him, and how she had saved his life. "Ah," said Grandpere, "there were women in those days!" And as he sighed and shook his white head, the four men rose and drank a standing toast to the women of yesteryear, forgetting all about little "Never-a-Care."

But there were tears in her eyes as she thought how little she was, and how useless in her "Never-a-Care" world, when there were big things to do all about her. She slipped out and went to her room and fell on the bed in a torrent of weeping. Then she sat up. She tore up the flowers and the dance-orders and stamped on them; and she threw the hateful box of bon bons into the corner.

The four old veterans were still in the library telling of the horrors of '70, when she walked in and told them that she was going to Europe to join the Red Cross, that she would show them that there were women *today!*

There was an awful fuss from Grandpere. "Nom de Dieu," it was not to be thought of; and the others were astonished and incredulous; but she was deaf to protest and entreaty. And the three veterans left, with Grandpere sitting with his white head bowed upon his breast, and "Never-a-Care" at his feet, tearful, but resolute.

They made a pet of her in the field — the

great, bearded, muddy soldiers. And she did her duty well. One young officer, Captain Hayward, swore to *that,* after she had bound up a trivial wound in his arm while he looked into her face. He had to have her attend to it very often — though he never paid any attention to it when he was with his fellows.

And then, at night, while the grim soldiers smoked their pipes in the glow of the campfires, she sang to them — " It's a long, long way to Tipperary.'' Maybe the tears didn't roll down their cheeks as they cheered!

As the days went by, Hayward and Celeste wound closer and closer about themselves that impalpable bond that binds lovers, until they knew. Then came the crash of arms and the bursting of shells. They brought in the wounded, and she ministered to them. She looked for Hayward, but he did not come. The colonel only shook his head and turned away when she asked about him. At night, she crept across the field among the dead. Shells burst around her at intervals.

She found him by the trenches, and he knew her. She knelt beside him, and his head was upon her bosom as he crossed over. She kissed his cold lips, and laid his head gently down. She rose, the frenzy of the bereaved tigress in her eyes — little " Never-a-Care! '' She stripped the Red Cross from her arm and the nurse's mantle from her breast. She took his sword and faced — GERMANY! And then the heavens were split apart; and when the smoke and dust had cleared away, little " Never-a-Care " lay across the body of Hayward, the sword in her hand.

THE HOUSE NEXT DOOR

Produced under title,
"The Professor's Romance."

Produced by The Vitagraph Company of America.

Featuring SIDNEY DREW.

Directed by Sidney Drew.

For more than ten years, the housekeeper had
opened the library door at exactly thirty minutes
past six, and announced that supper was ready.
And the Professor would close the volume —
Humboldt's Cosmos or Kant's Critique of Pure
Reason — put the book carefully back in its
place, pocket his glasses, and follow her into
the little dining room for his toast and tea
and canned peaches. The serenity of his bachelor household and its clock-like regularity had
been undisturbed for years. About his only
callers were the male members of The Society
for Ethical Research, who came to sit at the
feet of this Gamaliel, and drink in the words
that fell from his lips.

The Professor was " gun-shy " when it came

to the ladies. No romance had ever rippled the
calm of his methodical life; there was nothing
about dimples or star-eyes or ringlets in any of
the text-books he had either written or read, and
a picture of a heart looked to him like a conic
plane, attenuated at the apex, and with a curvi-
linear indented base. His interest in Venus was
confined to the theories in regard to the missing
arms of the Milo variety, and the way to differ-
entiate the Fourth Avenue antiques from the
ones Schliemann dug up at the Campanile or the
Acropolis — or somewhere. He could translate
the heiroglyphs on the sarcophagus of Cleopatra,
and tell you how she was mummified differently
from Ptolemy II., and that let him out about the
lady. All of which is pertinent to this story.

The house next door had a new tenant. Louise
had taken it for the summer, and had arrived
with Bill, and Elizabeth, and a dog and a nurse;
and forthwith the serenity of the Professor
departed. A low fence separated the two cot-
tages; but no fence was ever built that would
keep out Bill and Elizabeth when they had once
made up their minds to get on the other side.
They soon had a picket pried loose, and went
in and out as they listed.

Any dignified man who wears an out-of-date
silk hat and a very long frock coat is a natural
mark and a perpetual temptation to children like

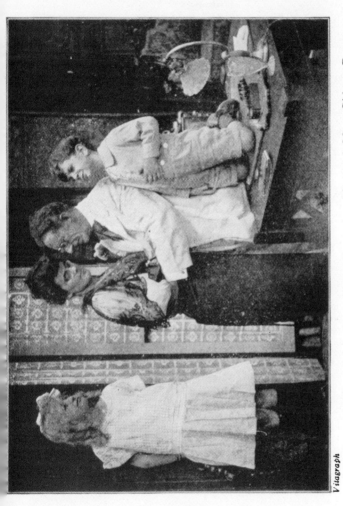

Vitagraph

From "The Professor's Romance"—Featuring Mr. and Mrs. Sidney Drew
and Bobby Connelly

that pair. They broke his windows and dispersed the meetings for the furtherance of Ethical Research. They ran the gamut of annoyance, until his deductions became faulty and his conclusions illogical — it is difficult to reason accurately when in fear of a half-brick or the water from a garden hose. He had to listen to the piano as played by Louise, and it drove him to shut the windows and put on ear-muffs.

And as he walked one day in the cool of the afternoon, beneath his own vine and fig tree, reading something light in the original Sanskrit, by way of recreation, a deluge of water from the hose overwhelmed him. As soon as he could gather his dripping senses and his glasses, he grabbed the pair and hustled them to their mother; and — fie upon her — when she saw him she laughed!

Now, when Louise laughed, anybody else laughed too, and that is exactly what the Professor did. Louise took him into the drawing room and spread a mackintosh over a chair and sat him on it, and made him drink some whiskey, after he had made a forcible but ineffectual protest. She spoke sadly of the children, and making little dabs at her eyes with a lace handkerchief, told him that they needed the firm hand of a father.

The Professor thought so too, but said it was

a mere nothing and didn't matter in the least. And that evening, as he sat with his feet in a mustard bath, with a blanket wrapped around the rest of him, the telephone rang — it was Louise inquiring if he had taken cold — and he told her, catarrhally, " Do, dot a bit. I have dot suffered ady idcodvediedce " — and went back and put his feet in the mustard bath, and smiled!

And a few evenings later, after he had arranged his hair for the eleventh time, he went out and talked to Louise over the fence for a few moments. When she went in, he saw that the moon was beautiful. He had always thought of it before as a cold satellite of the earth, without atmosphere, and the radius of whose orbit was 240,000 miles.

He sat in the library, and the music from the piano came tinkling through the window; old Mary, the housekeeper, brought the ear-muffs and shut the windows. But he discarded the ear-muffs as soon as she had gone, and softly opened all the windows, and sat with clasped hands, beating time with his foot.

As he glanced through the window the next day, he saw a man, dressed in the height of fashion, enter Louise's gate and ring her bell. For the first time in many years, he realized that his clothes were not exactly in style. A visit to the tailor and the hatter and the haberdasher and the boot-maker soon fixed that, and arrayed like Sullivan in all his glory, he emerged from the chrysalis of his sombre vesture, and almost scared old Mary to death when she saw him.

He called on Louise, and the kids " didn't do a thing to him." And Louise told him that they needed the firm hand of a father. He offered to assist her in any way that he could — and Louise sighed, wistfully. He bought an authority on the bringing up and control of children, by Miss S. P. Inster; and when " mother's angels " did something particularly outrageous, he consulted the book — and always found that " Children should never be spanked."

But after they had stolen his outing flannels and Mary's best dress from the line for a dress parade, and had pulled the plug out of the boat in which he took Louise boating, compelling them to wade ashore, and had done other ingeniously devilish things, he told Louise that " he was inclined to doubt the accuracy of the dogma as laid down in Miss S. P. Inster's book." And Louise said, " They need the firm hand of a father." He placidly admitted that that was so, and again Louise sighed.

But even the most bashful of men comes to taw at last. He sat with Louise on the sofa in her drawing room, and had laid his hand on his heart, and had swallowed hard several times, when the awful knowledge was borne in upon him that somebody was under the sofa — and he dragged out Elizabeth and Bill. He started to consult the book — but closed it, and taking Bill across his knee, spanked him with it heartily. Bill finally wriggled out of his grasp, and he and Elizabeth were sent to bed. Louise told him that " The children needed the firm hand of a father " — and after thinking a moment, he held up his good right hand and asked her if she thought it would do. She fell on his neck — being taken so by surprise!

Together they went later, to the nursery. There lay Elizabeth and Bill, tucked safe in their little beds, their sweet, gentle, child-faces dewy with the beauty sleep. Tenderly Louise kissed them, and the Professor, smiling, followed suit. He put his arm around Louise, and they softly went out. Then Bill and Elizabeth sat up in bed and winked at each other.

Vitagraph "*The Professor's Romance*"—*Featuring Mr. and Mrs. Sidney Drew*

THE MAKING-OVER OF GEOFFREY MANNING

Produced by The Vitagraph Company of America.

Featuring HARRY MOREY.

Directed by Harry Davenport.

A pussy-footed Jap glided noiselessly into the darkened bedroom, and cautiously pulled aside the silken hangings from the window, admitting the light. Geoffrey rolled over and yawned and opened his eyes. The little clock pointed at ten-thirty. He signed to the Jap to prepare his bath, and sat up aimlessly.

Of splendid physique and brilliant mind and innate refinement; of unquestioned social position and colossal fortune, the man had idled away his thirty-five years in the languid pursuit of ease and pleasure along the path of least resistance, wherein tread so many of his kind. Relieved of any necessity for work, or of any thought for the morrow, he had given his tastes full and free rein — books, art, travel — seldom dissipation — and had come, as is inevitable with such men, to regard himself as a trifle more than common clay, and scarcely subject to the limitations which circumscribe the " average man."

One morning he sat in his big six-cylinder, which he had stopped at the mill to drop Compton, his father's secretary (he had never been inside the mill himself), and witnessed a remarkable demonstration by his father's employees who felt that their rights had been violated by some cut in wages or increase in hours, and coolly asked Compton why he didn't have them shot. It was difficult for him to understand that these men had any rights which should be allowed to interfere with him in any way. Compton told him some plain truths, that not only surprised him, but made him feel decidedly uncomfortable.

That afternoon at the club, he got a second jolt. In a discussion of social conditions around a table in the grill room, a young " uplifter " told him that he, Geoffrey Manning, was of no real account in the world, and that he could not, stripped of the prestige of his name and money, and with nothing but his brain and his hands, accomplish anything worthy of note. Geoffrey thought the man talked like a fool, and told him so; but the iron had entered his soul. The idea that he, Geoffrey Manning, should be thought the inferior of any man, in any way!

He dined that evening with his father, one of the iron and coal barons — a gruff old wheel-horse who had long since given up all idea that Geoffrey would succeed him except as the legatee of his holdings — and Geoffrey, venturing an opinion on some industrial problem, was made to feel that the opinion of a bystander in the world's affairs wasn't worth three hoots in any place. Jar number three — all in one day!

Now, Geoffrey was by no means a fool, and his family had no branch that was weak or without pride; and he began to wonder if these people were right, and whether he did, after all, measure up to the stature of a man. There was one way to find out — to put himself to the test! And Geoffrey thought a long time that night; and the longer he thought, the firmer his jaw set; and when the pussy-footed Jap came in the next morning, he found the bed untouched and his master gone; and he shuffled out again solemnly, as is the way of well-trained Japs.

Geoffrey took one man into his confidence — old Mr. Mathews, his father's attorney, and arranged that if he communicated with him, Mathews was to follow out instructions to the letter. He told his father he was going to shoot elephants in Africa, or something; but the old man didn't care whether he shot elephants in Africa or craps in Mobile, being busily engaged, just then, in sand-bagging a rival concern that had the temerity to enter into competition with him.

He wrote Margaret Maxwell, to whom it had been tacitly understood he would be married some day, that he was going away indefinitely. Margaret was of his own emotionless class. She shrugged her aristocratic shoulders; " she could wait, or, if anyone else came along, whose rating was good at Bradstreet's, she would take *him*." There was no nonsense about Margaret.

So Geoffrey disappeared completely — the ways are many and easy — and in twenty-four hours, he faced the world in a flannel shirt and a cheap suit of clothes, with a five dollar bill in his pocket! He stood on a corner in a part of the town he didn't remember having seen before, and wondered what to do first. He watched the heterogeneous tide pass him, and he wondered what they all did. He bought a couple of papers and went into the little park to read the " want ads." He found the benches filled with derelicts and others, and he rather resented it that someone did not get up and give him a seat. He found one at last, and he searched the columns, tearing out several that he thought looked promising, and throwing the torn papers on to the walk. A big policeman came and told him to pick them up and put them into the refuse can. After some hesitation, he did as he was told.

The afternoon was getting on; one must have a base of operations; he would find a comfortable room and start out in the morning. He walked leisurely through the streets that have " E " in front of them, looking for a suitable place among the many dubious houses that bore the little card — " Furnished Rooms."

As he mounted the steps of one that seemed a little less run-down-at-the-heels than the others, a girl carrying a music-roll ran past him, and taking a latch-key from her purse, opened the door, and turned to him inquiringly. He asked for the landlady, and the girl called her, and then ran up the stairs. He hesitated between a coffin-like hall-bedroom, at a dollar-fifty a week, and a square room, at three dollars; and though the three would put quite a dent in his five dollars, he couldn't altogether overcome the habit of years, so he paid the three for the comparative luxury. As he sat in his room, he felt for the first time in years, the joy of responsibility that a man of strong mind and body feels when put upon his own resources; and he slept well, after a carefully ordered dinner in a " beanery," that reduced his capital to about a dollar and a half.

In the morning, he took the " ads." that he had torn from the papers, and started out to find work. Suffice it to say that he couldn't find it — he must have experience here, he must know the trade there; he was too young, or too old, etc., etc. And he went home tired and hungry, and ate his capital down to sixty cents.

As he sat in his room, there came to him from the room adjoining, the clear, beautiful notes of a woman's voice — Aida in East Twelfth Street! He listened and knew that the voice was no ordinary one. Somehow, he knew it was the girl with the music-roll that he had met on the steps. She sang many times during the evening, and he was sorry when she stopped; but he was tired and fell into a dreamless sleep — tomorrow something *must* be done.

Tomorrow saw the last of his money go, and no work was in sight. He saw men at work with pick and shovel in the street, and it actually looked attractive to him. As he got hungrier, he remembered the bread-line that he had watched with idle curiosity from the twelve-inch upholstery of his automobile. But he had decided to play the game; and if this was a part of it, he would play it. He heard the songs again that evening, and was soothed and comforted by the music.

The next morning, he applied for work to the

boss of a gang that was tearing up a street, and the boss looked over his big frame, and took him on by the day. After an hour of it, it seemed as though he could stand it no longer; but he had made up his mind to go through with it, and he did. Margaret Maxwell and two of his friends drove past in a motor-car, but of course did not recognize him, although the car stopped within a few feet of him, and he leaned on his shovel and looked straight at them. Flanagan, the boss, swore at him for " soldiering," and Geoffrey resumed his work. When night came, he got his slip for one dollar and sixty-five cents — the first money he had ever earned! He was sore and stiff, and glad of it! He had proved that he *could* work, anyhow. She did not sing that night, and he felt disappointed.

He worked three days; and then, when Flanagan got particularly abusive to a much smaller man, Geoffrey knocked him down, and of course, was discharged. It was not easy to get another job, and he and Hennessy, the janitor, used to talk it over o' nights and exchange ideas on the state of the labor market. He met the girl, too, quite naturally, and they had pleasant little talks across the fire-escape that joined their windows, chaperoned by fire-escape parties above and below. He found that her name was Harmony Laurie, and that she taught music that

she might study it, and that she was going to
be a great singer if she could. That she had
gray eyes and brown hair, and believed she had
a " future "——

And he thought so too. He resolved to help
her toward her ambition. He wrote to Lawyer
Mathews about it secretly; and one evening,
Harmony told him enthusiastically that she had
had a fine choir position offered her — and he
never let her suspect that he was at the bottom
of it. She said he must come to hear her sing.
He went — his first appearance in church in some
years — and he was very glad he went.

One evening, Hennessy told him that good
jobs were to be had at Old Man Manning's mill
— the last strike had made many vacancies.
Work in the mill of his father! Why not? The
very irony of the thing attracted him. He
applied, of course unrecognized, and was taken
on. He trucked pig-iron until one day he made
a suggestion to the foreman that showed he was
intelligent and interested in his work; the suggestion was adopted, and he was advanced. He
stood now at one of the blazing forges, grimy
of hand and face, bare armed and bare chested,
with leather apron, and swung a heavy sledge
with mighty blows upon the hot metal.

One day, his father escorted some visitors
through the mill. Geoffrey knew several in the

Vitagraph
Harry T. Morey and Thomas Mills in "The Making Over of Geoffrey Manning"

party; but no one suspected that the grimy giant was Geoffrey Manning, and he didn't inform them. Old Man Manning noticed him and inquired about him, and the foreman told him that the giant was a man by the name of Hunter, and that he was the best man in the works. Mr. Manning grunted, and went off with his party.

Indeed, the men in the mill had begun to look up to him; he attended their meetings and was interested in their affairs. He saw their homes; he saw their needs and their wrongs as they saw them; for was he not one of them? He was being made over as the iron is made over in a Bessemer converter. He looked on them now, not as cogs in the wheel — not as mere units in a system that was made for his benefit — but as sentient beings, heads of families, each having his own place in the world.

And all the while, he and Harmony drew closer together. When he spent an evening without seeing her or hearing her sing, he felt uncomfortable and incomplete. Then came the trouble at the mill — the very industrial air was full of strikes and discontent, and John Manning was a hard man to give in to labor's demands. The men decided that Geoffrey should present their case. He told them it was impossible; he could not face his father then without revealing

his identity, and he wasn't ready for that by a
long way. But they insisted, and he went home
that night to think it over.

Harmony was all in a flutter — she had been
asked to sing at the Charity Bazaar — a func-
tion of the elect, for fashionable giving. He
must go, she said. He looked at himself in the
glass; his flesh hung no longer in flabby folds —
muscles had taken the place of them; his beard
was gone — no one would know him. He called
up Togo, and Togo came with the evening
clothes — just as though it were part of the
day's routine. No one but Geoffrey could get
any information out of Togo, and his secret was
safe. Geoffrey stood among the elect again,
and many looked at him and searched the crannies of their memories, but they couldn't quite
" make him."

And Harmony sang beautifully. She and
Geoffrey went away together, Harmony feeling
a little awed and uncomfortable — he looked so
distinguished — but she was happy withal.

A block from home, Geoffrey darted out into
the street and pulled a waif from under the
wheels of a passing " joy-rider;" and when
they picked him up from the gutter, it didn't
look as though he would ever be of much account
again. For many days he lay and babbled of
the mill and of Harmony and " father," and for

many days, Harmony watched and prayed beside him. Finally his strong body and his clean living won out, and the light of reason came again into his eyes; — reason, and something else, too.

He went back to the mill and the trouble was still troubling. He felt strong enough now to take up their cause with his father. He went into the office — the beard had grown — and his father knew him. As he told the men's story and pleaded their cause, the scales fell from the Old Man's eyes, and he knew the whole truth. He recognized in his son the giant of the forge. This man whom all commended, and on whom all leaned, was his son — no longer the idler and the Sybarite, but the tower of strength and reliance he had pictured *his* son *should* be! That was one strike the men won, anyhow.

And Harmony — Geoffrey and the Old Man fooled her scandalously! After the wedding in the Rev. Mr. Hollywell's study, at which the witnesses were Hennessy (who allowed as how he was the best man) and an old man in white side-whiskers, who wore rough clothes and who was so excited that he kissed both the bride and groom, and gave Mr. Hollywell a thousand dollar bill, they went to a house that Geoffrey told Harmony had been lent them for the honeymoon. She felt a little like Cinderella at the ball among the Persian carpets and tapestries and paintings and statuary and butlers and footmen and the Jap and the maids — all of whom seemed to know Geoffrey and the little old man with the white side-whiskers, who bossed everybody about as though he owned the place, and took such an interest in the bride and groom. And then Geoffrey had to go and call him " Father " — and the cat was out of the bag! And — but what's the use of telling it all?

When Geoffrey Manning, Jr., gets big enough, he will have a fine job learning the business of " John Manning & Son," and I take it he will have an inheritance better than that, too. Mental traits are handed down from father to son just as surely as bonds or blond hair; and the making-over of Geoffrey Manning will take off just that much of the handicap the youngster would have had, if his father had not put his soul on trial.

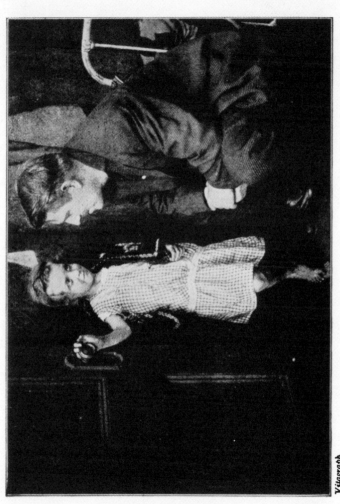

Harry T. Morey and Jacqueline Braun in "The Making Over of Geoffrey Manning"

THE LAW AND PEGGY

Produced by The Universal Film Company.

Featuring EDITH ROBERTS.

Among the many mortgages to which Hugh Travers fell heir at the death of his very wealthy father, was one upon " the house, lands, buildings, and all the contents thereof," belonging to one Dabney Fairfax, of Cloverdale. The mortgage was long past due, no interest having been paid upon it for years; and so Hugh, having some eye to business, in clearing up a lot of odds and ends of the estate, had the mortgage foreclosed, and took over the property, as there were no other bidders. For some reason, there seemed to be great delay in getting rid of the tenant who, Hugh was informed, was a Miss Fairfax; and so, Cloverdale being within easy motoring distance from the city, Hugh concluded to take a run down there and see about it.

As a matter of fact, the " tenant," Miss Fairfax, was exactly eighteen, just old enough to escape the nuisance of a legal guardian; but she had a very efficient and natural one in old

141

Mandy, who had been a " servant in the house " for more than a generation, and whose devotion to Peggy was a matter upon which there could be no doubt. Nominally a servant, she was really " boss of the outfit," and did the planning, and what little " financeering " there was — and that was really a good deal; for the Fairfax purse was exceedingly slender, and it required considerable tact and sagacity to " get by." Peggy's grandfather had left her, his only living kin, a fine little collection of debts and the old mortgaged home as a legacy; and now, by due process of law, the home had been sold out over Peggy's head under foreclosure to Hugh Travers, mortgagee, and he wanted possession.

Peggy and Mandy could not, of course, understand any process to be reasonable whereby they would be deprived of the home that had been in the family for more than a century, and so Peggy decided that she wouldn't leave it, law or no law. And in this she was backed up by the belligerent Mandy, to the mortal terror of those who had been there to serve the various kinds of papers that such a proceeding requires. Old Judge Harkness, who had been a friend of the Fairfaxes for fifty years, drove by in his old ramshackle buggy and stopped at the gate, where Peggy stood playing with a cat. She ran to the buggy and made the cat walk the wheel as they talked.

" You know, Honey," he said, " the old place is sold to that city chap. Where are you and Mandy aimin' to go? "

" We ain't aimin' to go no place," said the complaisant Peggy, " we are goin' to stay." Logic failed anybody in the presence of Peggy, and the old Judge shook his head and sighed sadly, and drove along. Let somebody else tell her all the unpleasant things which she must soon hear — he would not.

Of course, Hugh had never seen Peggy. He imagined the Miss Fairfax, who was the hold-over tenant that he was having so much trouble in getting out, to be a tall, gaunt old maid, probably too mean to pay anything she could avoid, and altogether a most undesirable and uncomfortable person.

He drove into Cloverdale in his big car, and stopped at the Judge's office. The Judge sat smoking a pipe, his coat off and his feet on the table, when Hugh came in and explained his errand; and with reluctance, the Judge began to draw the papers. The Sheriff and his Deputy, middle-aged men and long time friends of the Fairfaxes, stopped at the gate to talk to Peggy.

In the midst of the conversation, Hugh drove

by in his car, and almost broke his neck looking back at Peggy, who, by the way, nearly broke hers looking after him; all of which was seen by Mandy, and Peggy was forthwith ordered into the house.

As the Sheriff and his Deputy passed the Judge's office, the Judge leaned out of the window and called them in and gave them the papers in the case of Travers vs. Fairfax. He told them that they had all known the girl since infancy, and he knew how they hated to do it; but "the law's the law," said the Judge, and they'd have to do their duty. They took the papers and started toward the Fairfax home, looking for all the world like two truant school-boys about to follow father to the woodshed. Each tried to put it off on the other, and neither being willing, they concluded that misery loved company enough to go together. Mandy admitted them, grudgingly, and went to get Peggy, while they sat in the old fashioned parlor, nervous and uncomfortable. Peggy came in, and they handed her the papers and explained.

Mandy rolled up her sleeves belligerently. "Who say dat chile gotta get out? Le's see somebody jes' look like dey gwine put her out! Jes' le's see 'em! Dass all!" And the Deputy hastily pointed out that they were acting under the Judge's order, signed by him.

" Why, the very idea! " said Peggy. " How dare Judge Harkness do anything like that after we have entertained him here for years? " The Sheriff and the Deputy agreed, weakly, that it did seem strange; and after a little more talk, they left, each feeling like a criminal.

They had scarcely gone, when Hugh stood at the front door and knocked, and was finally admitted by the suspicious Mandy; and Peggy came demurely in.

Hugh looked at her and smiled pleasantly — " I asked for Miss Fairfax, the tenant here. I suppose she is your aunt — or something? "

Peggy explained that she was the only " Miss Fairfax," and the one against whom he had set the mighty machinery of the law in motion; and he felt more like a criminal than the Sheriff had. And as fast as his confused brain would let him, he told her that the lawyers had made a big mistake; and it took him so long to explain that he stayed to supper. And before they knew it — the moon was very bright that night — it was bedtime! Peggy wouldn't hear of his going to the hotel — in the first place, there wasn't any — and so it was arranged that he stay there for the night. He and Peggy were at the piano in the big, quaint, candle-lighted parlor, when Mandy came in with Peggy's candle in her hand and sent her off to bed. Peggy was reluctant to go, and indicated that Hugh must be taken care of.

" Yass'm," said Mandy, " I done 'range 'bout dat. De gen'lmun gwine to sleep in de barn." Peggy put up an awful kick, but Hugh hastened to assure her that he had intended doing that all the time; and finally Mandy led the way to the barn, a candle in her hand and bed-clothes in her arms, slammed up some straw in a corner, and flung down the bed-clothes. " Dar! " she said, laconically.

Hugh smiled, and thanking Mandy, he drew out a huge roll of bills and peeled off several and handed them to Mandy. Mandy gasped; and right there, her opinion of Hugh went up nine hundred per cent. She hastily and solicitously re-arranged the make-shift bed, and after thanking Hugh profusely, she went out chuckling.

Many times thereafter, Hugh's car drew up to the Fairfax door; and one day it stopped at the Judge's office. The Sheriff and the Deputy were there, and it cannot be said that Hugh's reception was cordial. But Hugh explained that if he had known anything of the circumstances, he would never have dreamed of trying to dispossess Peggy, and that he wanted the Judge to draw a lease, whereby Peggy might use the property as long as she paid to him one half of " the profits " of the farm. The Judge and the Sheriff and the Deputy got up and wrung Hugh's hand, and the Judge indignantly refused to take a cent for his services in the matter.

Armed with the lease, Hugh started back to the farm. Peggy had been thinking things over, and had come to the conclusion that it was all wrong for her to stay on another's property, and had finally convinced Mandy of it. They got together in the parlor a few of their most treasured possessions, including the cat, and when Hugh came in, he found them both tearful over the pitiful little heap of treasures.

" We know," said Peggy, " that everything in the house was sold with it, but Mandy and I thought maybe you would be willing to sell us these things — and the cat. Mandy has a little money."

Hugh hastily exhibited the lease and explained its terms. Mandy praised God loudly, and Peggy, in the excess of her joy, threw her arms about Hugh's neck and kissed him; then ran like a scared rabbit out of the room, shamefacedly. Mandy knelt down and kissed the hem of his garment; but Hugh was looking after Peggy. Mandy looked at Hugh and indicated that he would better find Peggy.

He went, and he finally cornered Peggy, who

held herself braced against the door to keep him out. He called to her — she took one hand away, then one or two fingers of the other, until, finally, the door was held against him by her little finger. And that is never strong enough to keep a big, eager man away from what he wants.

THE PASSING OF DUSTY RHODES

Produced by The Universal Film Company.

Featuring KING BAGGOT.

Directed by Mr. Webster.

His name was "Dusty Rhodes." At least, that is what his companions of the road called him. Among these gentry one name is as good as another, and no questions are asked about one's private affairs. He came swinging down the hilly country road toward the little town, looking the typical tramp, with fuzzy whiskers and dangling can. He saw no chalk-mark symbols, such as his kind are wont to leave in conspicuous places for the benefit of their fellows who may follow, and he tried his luck at the back door of a rather comfortable looking farm house. A kindly old lady brought him out a "knee-deep" pie and other things, such as he had not seen in years.

But the fairest prospects are sometimes deceptive, and even as he ate, a sour looking woman was telling the town constable that there was

a tramp in town down at Miss Peabody's. And
pointing to the placard that was pasted on the
outer walls of the post-office, giving notice, in
no uncertain terms, that all tramps would be
given a chance at the rock pile if they remained
in town more than fifteen minutes, she sharply
chided the peace officer on his neglect of duty.
And that worthy, seeing that his Colt .44 was in
good working order, and taking a firmer grasp
on his club, started in haste in the direction of
Miss Peabody's to uphold the majesty of the
law. He grabbed the good natured and unresisting Dusty just as he had finished the last of the
milk and pie, and hustled him down to the post-
office, much as the Caesars brought in their cap-
tives; and showing him the placard, while the
natives threatened and plagued, told Dusty to
be on his way and to beware his return. And
Dusty stood not on the order of his going,
though in a peaceful and dignified manner, and
as if there were no hurry about it.

Down the road he went, whistling and singing,
stopping only to pick a wild flower and put it
in his tattered coat. As night was falling, he
went into the woods, selected a suitable spot,
built himself a small fire by a big rock under
an overhanging tree, and settled down to roast
a few potatoes — a tramp can eat any time —
and to look into the glowing embers — there is

nothing like looking into glowing embers in the vast solitude of the woods for introspection.

Slowly visions of his past went before him in review — the failure of the bank, wherein were his savings, the pillaged safe that forced upon him the knowledge that his friend and partner had robbed him; the drowning of his wife and little daughter. And then the almost inevitable bottle for such natures as his, and the rapid descent into lost ambitions and inebriety. And finally, here he was, a tramp, kicked out of town and shunned like a pestilence. When he came to, his potatoes were charred, but he only shrugged his shoulders and composed himself for sleep.

And as he and the village slept in fancied security, the logs that the lumbermen had cut for many days in the winter and spring and had set adrift in the river above the town, came swirling down with the current, until, in an unlucky moment, one of them caught and held the others as they came, and the dreaded log-jam of the lumber towns was a reality! Just as the dawn was breaking, a frantic man climbed dripping from the river and ran through the town giving the alarm and calling all men to help. They came to the river bank and looked upon the thundering waters and the perilous task that confronted them.

Dusty heard the tumult and came too. Hemmed in the steep gorge of the river, their homes and their all were imperiled. It was almost certain death to try to break the jam. The constable was there, and the postmaster, and the squire, and the town bully — but none of them wanted the job, though women wept and prayed and begged them to try. It was a man's job, and Dusty took it. He stripped off his coat and shoes, and grasping an axe and a pike, he went into the angry waters. He slipped a dozen times in the boiling torrent and the treacherous logs and the blinding spray, while the hearts of the watchers sank in their bosoms and it seemed impossible that he could reach the "key-log." But he made it, and with powerful blows he cut it away, and the mass tottered, swayed, groaned, and fell, as Dusty leaped for safety. Too late. And as the women covered their faces, he rolled from the logs into the black waters, and to — Heaven, is my guess.

And when the men sat before the post-office and talked it over — they weren't any too proud of themselves. Old Miss Peabody came — she who had given him the pie and the milk at her door — and looked them over as though she didn't see anything in particular, and ripped off the placard from the post-office wall that gave warning to all tramps, and tore it into bits.

And if you will go up behind the village to the spot they still call " God's Acre " in that part of New England, you will see a rude memorial to an unknown man who gave his life that others might live.

THE SOCIAL ADVENTURES OF LORD NOCASTLE

In production by The Edison Company.

The matutinal "tub" was evidently in splashy progress, and from behind the screen in Lord Nocastle's modest lodgings, in a genteel but not exclusive part of London, came heart-rending shrieks for a towel. Gubbins, his man, who was quietly helping himself to a portion of the contents of a decanter which stood on the table, was so startled that he spilled most of it, almost strangled on the rest, and dropped the glass, but sprang away on a frantic hunt for that very necessary article. Around the side of the screen protruded the wet head, shoulder, and arm of His Lordship, as he urged the clumsy and rattled Gubbins to greater speed and efficiency. It was of no use — there didn't seem to be any towels; and as a substitute, Gubbins snatched a huge fur motoring coat from a closet, and draped it over the shivering shoulders of the nobleman.

All this time, an insistent and authoritative

knocking was going on at the door of the outer
room; and Gubbins, in his agitation, upset the
screen; and there, in a little tin tub, sat the
next in succession to the title, with about one
hundred and eighty dollars' worth of fur over-
coat draped tastefully about him. Gubbins
replaced the screen about the outraged nobleman,
and hurried to the door. There stood the huge
and belligerent Mr. Small, a most insistent and
annoying creditor of His Lordship, with two
other individuals who simply had accounts to
collect.

Mr. Small had every appearance of a man
who was about to commit mayhem, or something
equally unpleasant. The two inoffensive col-
lectors, arriving at the same moment as Mr.
Small, shrank within themselves every time he
glared at them, and backed up a little. Gubbins
explained to Mr. Small — he paid no attention
to the other men — that he had called at a most
inopportune time, and that if he would wait a
little, His Lordship would undoubtedly adjust
the account. This did not seem at all satisfac-
tory to Mr. Small, who said that he would wait —
on the front steps — and see His Lordship in
person; and on the steps he proceeded to seat
himself. The two other men concluded to wait
also, but to stand. But after Mr. Small had
looked at them a couple of times, they concluded

to " call it a day," and left, leaving the field entirely to Mr. Small.

By the time Gubbins got His Lordship partially dressed, the landlady came in with the breakfast and the mail; and between buttoning His Lordship's collar and opening the eggs, Gubbins had considerable difficulty in keeping the two apart, not having recovered from the daily shock administered to him by the belligerent Mr. Small. Finally, as His Lordship was pulling on his gloves preparatory to departing, Gubbins ventured to remind him that Mr. Small was still seated on the front steps; and added, " beggin' 'is Ludship's pawdon," that " it seemed 'ighly necessary that 'is Ludship see 'is huncle, the Hearl, and hobtain sufficient money to happease this quite ferocious Mr. Small. 'E's a bit of a wrong 'un! Hi quite fear for me life, beggin' Your Ludship's pawdon! "

As a precautionary measure, Nocastle took a peek out of the window, and sure enough, there sat Mr. Small upon the steps! His Lordship, after deliberation, decided to postpone his departure, for the time being.

Then and there arose the loyal soul of Gubbins. It was entirely necessary that His Lordship get out of the house and see his uncle, " the Hearl." Gubbins put on his hat and coat and

stole softly down the stairs and opened the door.
The broad expanse of Mr. Small's back almost
filled the steps. Gubbins took a hitch in his
trousers and swallowed hard a couple of times,
and then, dashing past Mr. Small, he jammed
that gentleman's hat down upon his eyes so
hard, that by the time Mr. Small had pried his
head out of it, Gubbins had at least fifteen feet
start, which was not an inch too much; for Mr.
Small took up the chase with surprising agility
for a man of his size.

But the ruse succeeded, and whatever the fate
of the loyal Gubbins, Lord Nocastle came out of
his lodgings with the leisurely and unconcerned
air that befitted his station, even pausing on the
steps to light a cigarette; all of which would
have been impossible except for the self-immola-
tion of the devoted Gubbins. His Lordship came
into his uncle's library unannounced, and found
the old gentleman chuckling over something
which he manifestly tried to conceal, with more
or less success.

The old Earl knew exactly what was coming,
and before His Lordship had got well started
in his story, the Earl held up a protesting hand
— " Spare me the awful and harrowing details —
how much? " " Two hundred pounds," said his
nephew, a trifle uncertainly. This brought forth
an apoplectic roar from the old man, and Lord

Nocastle amended, hastily, "One hundred."
This was like a back tooth, but the Earl turned
to his desk to write the cheque. His Lordship,
deeming it best to let well enough alone, shut
up like a clam; but stepping over to the table,
he saw thereon a long, white kid glove! He
adjusted his monocle and examined it; and it
was only with the greatest presence of mind
that he restrained himself from saying, "My
word!"

The Earl handed him the hastily scribbled
cheque, and his demeanor toward his nephew
was so unmistakably that of a man who wants
to be alone that Lord Nocastle mumbled his
perfunctory thanks and went out wondering.
He arrived at the club almost at the same
moment as the perspiring Gubbins, Mr. Small
having finally given up the pursuit, with certain
remarks about what he would do the next time
he met him. There was considerable method in
Gubbin's madness, for he knew that if any part
of Uncle's cheque were to be applied to alleviat-
ing the strain at the lodging, he would better
meet Lord Nocastle going *into* the club, rather
than coming out.

And indeed, Gubbin's apprehension was jus-
tified, for at the moment when he was reaching
for the cheque, Lord Nocastle having indorsed
it, a fellow member came down the steps, look-

ing very dejected about something, and told His Lordship what a bally mess he was in and how he jolly well needed a hundred pounds to get him out of it. And when Nocastle sympathized with the man and gave him the cheque and went back into the club with him, Gubbins collapsed, and felt that Love's labors are indeed lost, at times!

Mlle. Fifi LeClaire (nee Katie Cleary) was the rage of The Follies Parisienne. And when she shooed a bunch of Johnnies out of her dressing room, telling them, as well as she could on account of the shrieks of laughter, some of which was her own, that she was going to be married, not one of them believed her. But Mlle. Fifi was over seven and would not tear under the wing, and she knew, all the time, exactly how many beans made six — which being interpreted means, that she had been graduated from the broiler class and was wise in her day and generation.

She took up from her table a bunch of roses that must have cost about nine thousand kopecks, and smuggled her nose into them and laughed. She looked at a card that was attached to the bunch, and laughed again, louder than ever, and proceeded to dress for the evening performance.

It was very dull at the club, and somebody proposed that they go to see Fifi; Lord Nocastle didn't really want to go, but they dragged him to it. And from one of the boxes, he got his first look at Fifi, and was not particularly impressed. Fifi devoted all her attention to, and played exclusively for, someone in a closely curtained lower box opposite to them. Lord Nocastle's companions nearly broke their necks trying to see who was in the box, but were unable to do so; and after the show, it was proposed that they go back of the stage to see her and to learn why she had deserted them. Nocastle refused to do this, and got into a cab instead, headed for his lodgings. At a congested point, a big limousine was held up for a moment alongside of him and he got a good look at its occupants before it drew away. In the limousine were his uncle, the Earl of Popham, and Mlle. Fifi LeClaire! "My word!" said Lord Nocastle.

Gubbins brought the morning papers to His Lordship as he sat up in bed and sipped his cocoa. There were scare headlines which said that the aged Earl of Popham had made Mlle. Fifi LeClaire his Countess the day before! The faithful Gubbins collapsed into a state of semi-coma; but His Lordship never turned a hair. At the club, the reporters asked him about the affair and showed him the newspaper accounts. Lord Nocastle adjusted his monocle with care and precision and looked casually at the article.

" Aw," he said, calmly, " The Earl of Popham,
you mean? Really, he is no longer an uncle of
mine. I have cast him off! "

Months went by, and it came about that one
fine morning, as he walked in Rotten Row with
a club friend, Nocastle met some Americans. A
tall and very beautiful girl was driving a slash-
ing pair, and the whole turnout attracted much
attention. Beside the girl sat a young man who
had " Fifth Avenue, Manhattan, U. S. A."
stamped all over him. The girl nodded brightly
to Lord Nocastle's companion, and drew up the
horses, and in due course, His Lordship was
presented to Helen and Larry.

Nocastle never once took his eyes off the girl.
" Who is she? " he asked, when they had finally
driven off?

" That is Miss Juggins," said his friend. " The
daughter of Juggins Soap of America, or something. No end of money, and all that, doncher-
know! And quite ripping! My word! What? "

Later that night, when he and his friend sat
over their whiskey and water in Nocastle's
rooms, his friend said, " I say, old chap, why
don't you have a run over to America and all
that? Some of our chaps have done rawther
well over there. What? " And the more His
Lordship thought the matter over, the more
attractive it seemed.

The Countess of Popham, formerly Fifi Le-Claire, was entertaining that evening — just a few friends from the Follies Parisienne who had dropped in casually — and they had quite a pleasant evening, losing most of their awe for the nobility after the sixth drink, and after they had found out that the gorgeous individual in livery wasn't " the Hearl.'' The Countess was quite her old self, and mixed the drinks on the piano, and played for them to dance. In fact, she did a little dancing herself, just to show them that she hadn't forgotten. " Bli'me," said one of the guests, " bein' a bloomin' nabob 'asn't chainged 'er a bit! "

The " Hearl " was beginning to feel that way about it, too. He sat in the library and listened to the bric-a-brac break, as several of the guests showed a little of their stuff in acrobatic and juggler specialties. And the Countess was a good deal put out about it when the Earl stamped in and ordered them all out of the house. They went, after considerable debate, the Countess having countermanded the Earl's order; but they all promised to come again. Some of the gentlemen, as well as all the ladies, insisted on kissing the Earl affectionately at parting! What saved the old man from apoplexy is a mystery.

And it was just about this time, that Lord

Nocastle, having turned the matter of America over in his mind, rose and said to the apprehensive Gubbins, " Pack the luggage! We shall sail for America — if I can borrow the money. I quite wonder what boat that Miss Juggins is taking? "

The dining room in the Fifth Avenue mansion of J. Hooper Juggins, was a trifle smaller than the Polo Grounds, and for the purpose of dining, it was just about as comfortable. It was here that J. Hooper received instruction in table etiquette from Mrs. J. Hooper and a most impressive butler, at meals. It was a part of the duty of the butler to guide the erring feet of the Juggins family along the somewhat difficult path of Swelldom's good form. He was eminently fitted for the job, for had he not buttled for a family worth at least six millions more than J. Hooper? Quite so!

J. Hooper Juggins used to be John H. Juggins when he had a soap-works over in Hoboken, and was piling up his millions. At that time, John H. Juggins considered himself quite a man, with a strong and aggressive personality; it was well known that " he could talk to truck-drivers in their own language." Under the enervating influence of the atmosphere of plutocracy, however, J. Hooper Juggins lost much of the assertive nature of John H., and acquired that of a

tame rabbit, always conscious that he was doing
something he ought not to. His mistakes at
table were pointed out by Mrs. Juggins, who
usually used a fork or a stick of celery as a
pointer. The butler called attention to his trans-
gressions, and to those of Mrs. Juggins as well,
by coughing behind his hand; which manner of
correction was so incessant that it threatened to
result in an affection of the throat.

J. Hooper was usually very tolerant and amen-
able to these corrections, wincing and starting
guiltily, with a sort of "Now-what-have-I-
done?" air. But at times, he would kick over
the traces, slam down his napkin, and retreat
to the sanctuary of the library, where he was
allowed some latitude. Removing his coat and
boots, and assuring himself that the argus-eyed
butler was not spying, he would light a very dis-
reputable and smelly pipe, take from the bookcase a section of pasteboard which was painted
to represent the backs of books, and which concealed a black bottle and two glasses, and pro-
ceed to enjoy himself. If there happened to be
company, the butler came in and made him put
out the pipe and put on his coat and boots —
he was always careful to conceal the black bottle
himself. Frequently, the butler returned to the
dining room to find Mrs. Juggins pouring her
coffee into the saucer, and he would cough in a

most distressed manner; and Mrs. Juggins would pour the coffee back into the cup apologetically, and drink it with the air of a duchess.

It was toward this household, on the same boat with Helen and Larry Juggins, that Lord Nocastle was headed. Among those on the pier to see him off was Mr. Small, who had recovered his belligerency; but he was just late enough to see the boat slip out into the stream, and to be mocked by the safe and exultant Gubbins.

The trip was somewhat eventful, Gubbins being very ill most of the way, which fact threatened to keep Lord Nocastle in bed, as he had the utmost difficulty in dressing himself; and probably never would have accomplished it, but for a steward who responded to his S. O. S. Incidentally, Lord Nocastle exposed a couple of " Deep Sea Fishermen," who had Larry well hooked in a poker game, by turning up the table and revealing a small but efficient " bug " which one of them was using, at intervals, to strengthen his hand. This episode, together with the fact that he was most entertaining on moonlight nights, when he and Helen paced the deck or sat in the steamer chairs, made him pretty solid with the Juggins family. And when the big ship landed, he rode in their Mercedes to the portals of the St. Croesus Hotel, where " Ma " Juggins advised him, by all means, to stay!— little knowing that his monthly cheque from the solicitors was for the sum of twenty pounds!

His stay there was not altogether happy, as may be imagined. He ignored the glistening porcelain bath-tub, and used the little tin affair that he had brought with him, the patient Gubbins filling it with a pitcher! In some way, the particular piece of " luggage " that contained his shirts was lost, and he and Gubbins were put to much inconvenience thereby. Toward the end of their stay, Gubbins had to do considerable laundry work, as " the blighter of a Chinaman " refused to give up the package without the money.

His first call at the Jugginses was eventful. Old Man Juggins was snoring sonorously in the library, and the sound was wafted across the hall to the drawing room. Mrs. Juggins sent the butler in with whispered orders to stop it at all hazards; — (" hazards " is right), for the Old Man woke in no very good humor. Before he could collect himself, the butler had invested him with his boots; but being thoroughly wakened by this process, he balked at his coat and insisted on having his pipe.

" 'Is Lordship is callin'," protested the butler, in awed and shocked whispers.

" To hell with His Lordship," shouted Juggins, " I want my pipe! " And he started toward the drawing room to get it, remembering that he had left it on the piano. The panic-stricken butler followed with his coat, and Mrs. Juggins frantically waved a staying hand through the draperies that separated the drawing room from the hall.

But Juggins was not to be denied; opposition only served to spur him on. He took a wallop at the butler who was trying to put on his coat, brushed aside the waving hand of Mrs. Juggins, and entered. " Hello, Duke," he said, " how's the King and Mrs. Pankhurst gettin' along these days? " Mrs. Juggins finally got him out, when he led the conversation toward a discussion of the soap business, and took him back into the library.

But when Lord Nocastle was leaving, and was alone in the hall with the butler, Juggins put his head out of the library and beckoned — " Psst! " Lord Nocastle went into the library, Juggins removed the pasteboard from the bookcase, got out the black bottle and the glasses. " I thought mebbe Your Countlets would like to hit up a couple of these here powders before you went. It's been a pretty dry evenin'."

And right there is where " His Countlets " made himself solid with Old Man Juggins. He sat down and " hit up " several, and discussed the soap business for two hours. He went, at last, after — " Just one more ' shock,'

Your Princeship! Jes' one little ole nightcap!
This ain't no third rail stuff!'' And they did.

The Old Man went to the door, with his arm
about Lord Nocastle's shoulder, pushed the butler out of the way, opened the door, pumped His
Lordship's hand hard, and told him to run in
any old time; and if he didn't happen to be there
he knew where to find the '' tonsil varnish!''
He closed the door and looked at the butler, who
retired hurriedly, and said, to himself, that he
'' guessed he'd hit the Ostermoor himself.''

Larry had been called on the telephone early
in the evening. On the other end of the wire
was Mrs. Knollys. At her side, in her fine apartment on The Drive, stood one Tony Martinez,
who was part of her entourge, and who '' framed
up '' schemes whereby she and he lived. This
time the '' good thing '' was Larry. He was
very willing to come; and he and Mrs. Knollys
spent a very pleasant evening; so pleasant, in
fact, that when Martinez came in, he found Mrs.
Knollys sitting very comfortably, smoking and
smiling. '' Nothing to it, Tony!'' she said,
blowing out a cloud of smoke. '' He is ripe
enough to be hand-picked. I'm going to *marry*
him!''

Things on the other side of the water had
come to a crisis between the old Earl and his
young wife. Long since, he had called in his

solicitors and bade them cut her out of his will as far as the law would let them — "Except of course, in case an heir should be born." And Fifi, listening at the door, made up her mind that that was exactly what was going to happen — heirs can be obtained almost anywhere, if one has the money and the nerve — and, Fifi had both, together with a large amount of unscrupulousness, and she proceeded to act accordingly.

Things were going kind of tough with Lord Nocastle and Gubbins at the St. Croesus; they didn't eat very regularly, for the remittance cheque was long overdue. Lord Nocastle dined frequently at the Juggins's, and managed to conceal food in his coat-tail pockets and bring it home to Gubbins, though once he forgot, and spent a most uncomfortable evening sitting on it. Then, again, on this day, Gubbins had put Lord Nocastle's only shirt into the bath-tub when the telephone rang. It was Larry, who insisted that His Lordship meet him and the prospective Mrs. Larry at Victor's for dinner. Lord Nocastle tried to get out of it, but couldn't. He looked at Gubbins, whose shirt was fresh laundered. Gubbins had got to be a mind-reader, these days, and started to peel off his shirt; and His Lordship kept the appointment.

He arrived at Victor's a little too early and took a seat at the table a little removed from

the body of the room. He saw Larry and Mrs.
Knollys come in and seat themselves, and then
Larry looked around, and finally saw him and
came to his table. While Larry had his back
turned to his own table, Lord Nocastle saw Tony
Martinez go quickly to Mrs. Knollys, slip a note
to her, and then very slyly kiss her and hurry
away. Larry didn't see this, but Lord Nocastle
made up his mind that the lady was no fit person
to become Mrs. Larry, and he proceeded to prove
it to the satisfaction of Larry by stealing the
lady from him and eventually getting possession
of the note.

But Larry didn't understand, and thought
Lord Nocastle was only taking his girl away
from him, and was very sore about it. He got
up from the table and left in a huff; and in a
moment more, the rest of the Juggins family
came into the restaurant, and Mrs. Juggins and
Helen spotted Lord Nocastle and Mrs. Knollys
seated over a bottle of wine, a previous bottle
of which had made the lady not only affectionate
in her demeanor toward His Lordship, but also
careless about who saw it. And the result was
that the Juggins family filed out, cutting Lord
Nocastle dead — except Old Man Juggins, who
winked violently at him as he passed. And in
the car, going home, he said, " You got to hand
it to his Dukeship for bein' a hot little sport

with the dames! My word! What? " And being duly sat on, he shut up, but continued to chuckle.

They wouldn't let Lord Nocastle explain; always at the Juggins mansion, they were " not at home." But Lord Nocastle sat in the St. Croesus and bided his time, knowing that it would all come out some day. In the darkest hour, when things couldn't be worse, they waited for the cheque, but feared to go to the door. An insistent knocking made Gubbins stand stock still and say " Shussh! " Then a big envelope came sliding under the door, and Gubbins grabbed it. Lord Nocastle opened it deliberately, read it, and then looked straight ahead, letting his hand fall limply. Gubbins took the cablegram and read it. It stated, very simply, that a son had been born to the Earl and Countess of Popham! And Gubbins collapsed in a heap on the floor! Gone were all the dreams, gone all hope!

Over in England, Fifi, with the aid and connivance of the doctor and a nurse, and by liberal use of money, had procured an heir to the Earldom, and it was easy to make the old Earl believe that it was his. But crime is weakness, and weakness always leaves something unprovided for. This time, it was Tony Martinez. The letter that Lord Nocastle had taken from Mrs. Knollys said that Tony had just discovered that his wife, who believed him dead, had been married to an English nobleman, and that the state of facts ought to make good picking for him, and that he was leaving for the other side. It advised Mrs. Knollys to marry the " sucker," and that he, Tony, would join her later. Tony made several ineffectual attempts to see his wife, and finally got desperate and climbed into her room from a balcony; whereat she promptly screamed, not recognizing him at first. This brought the Earl and several servants, with the result that when it was all over, Fifi had to confess that Tony was her lawful husband, and the nurse, who was rather a decent person and ashamed of her part in the deception, told how the baby had been procured. The shock was too much for the old Earl; and when the next day, the nurse came in with the baby to find what disposition was to be made of it, the Earl sat very white and still in the big library, and neither she nor the butler nor anyone else could wake him.

And then, in that even darker hour at the St. Croesus, came another message to " The Earl of Popham, formerly Viscount Nocastle." It said that the old Earl was dead, and that the circumstances preceeding his death made it certain that Lord Nocastle had come into the title. Gubbins danced and hoorayed. " You forget that my uncle is dead," reproved His Lordship. And Gubbins, abating not a jot in his merriment, said, " Beggin' your Lordship's pawdon, an' meanin' no disrespect to the former Hearl, I'm blime glad of it! "

Lord Nocastle and Gubbins sat in the ancestral library, and the butler had brought in *two* glasses with the bottle. Nocastle read a letter from Larry; it said that when they got his letter, they all understood his action, and Larry thanked God that Lord Nocastle had saved him from Mrs. Knollys and himself. (Old Man Juggins said that they ought to have known that His Majesty was a hot little sport) — and that they were all sailing on the first boat. Lord Nocastle raised his glass to clink with that of the tremulous Gubbins, when the nurse came timidly in with the baby and asked what should be done with it. His Lordship looked at it for a long time, and then reached out and took it. And as he clinked glasses with Gubbins, he dandled the baby on his knee.

A PAIR OF QUEENS

Produced by The Vitagraph Company of America.

Featuring FLORA FINCH, KATE PRICE,
HUGHEY MACK, and WILLIAM SHAY.

Directed by George Baker.

At seven-forty, on the morning after the ball of the Pants Pressers' Union, Local No. 21, the landlady knocked violently on the door of the girls' room — they were due at the store at eight. Mame and Sadie opened their eyes and looked at the clock in a startled, bewildered way, and then tumbled out of bed and into their clothes with all possible dispatch.

" Here's where the boss grabs off one swell little fine from we two," said Mame, as she wedged up her abundant back hair, and deftly fastened it with two hairpins. " Gee! This high society life is fierce! "

Mame was in the " Gents' Haberdashery," down at Pimpels, and Sadie held a steady job in the " Ladies' Shoes " at the same place. All they had to do was to stand behind a counter from eight A. M. until six P. M., six days a week, pull down upwards of a million boxes, and try on about the same number of shoes, and keep their tempers and be nice and pleasant. Then, every Saturday evening, they walked up to the cashier's cage, and that gentleman, with evident' unwillingness, not unmixed with an air of being convinced that they were taking money under false pretenses, reluctantly handed each an envelope in which there were six dollars — that is, six dollars, less the fines they had incurred during the week for various infractions of the rules. The fines ranged from five cents to one dollar. Then they had nothing to do until Monday morning! (And there are people who want to stop all forms of amusement on Sunday!)

They hustled down the front steps, putting on their jackets as they ran, and bidding a hasty " Good morning " to Hooligan, the iceman, who stood upon the sidewalk holding a very small piece of ice in a very large pair of tongs.

" Youse wrens is behind yer schedule," he grinned; " Throw her into high, and never mind the traffic cops, if ye want the store to open on time! " The girls stopped long enough at the stand on the corner to get a piece of chewing gum — for breakfast; and at six minutes after eight, the floor-walker said, cheerfully, " You are each fined twenty-five cents for being late! "

" What do you mean, late? " said Mame.

" Yes," said Sadie, " Where do you get that stuff? We was in the parcel room lookin' for a ' stray! ' "

" And five cents for impertinence," quoth the floor-walker. " You can't put nothing like that over on me. I seen you when you come in." And he walked over to Mazie's counter (Mazie was in the " Ladies' Hose ") and chucked her under the chin in a patronizing way. Someone had told him, once, that he looked like Earle Williams.

Mame followed him with wrathful eyes. " Say," she said to Lizzie, in the " Corsets," " Say! Did you get that? If that guy ever done that to me, I'd knock his block off! Me an' Sadie was to the Pants Pressers' Ball last night. One dead swell, elegant little affair, take it from me, Kid! An' perfect gents, them people are — there wasn't more'n three or four fights all evenin' — hardly! We gets nicked thirty cents by this here Francis X. Bushman just now for bein' late; but believe me, it was worth it! " And Mame turned languidly to half-a-dozen women customers who purchased 14½ collars for husbands with 16 necks. (Why not? Wasn't it " a sale? ")

Sadie fitted a pair of 4-A shoes on a two hundred pound woman with a 6-D foot. " If you

Vitagraph

Flora Finch in "A Pair of Queens"

find them a little large, Madam," said Sadie, with consummate saleswomanship, "I can put an insole in 'em for you, but they look somethin' grand on you! Mary Garden always gets them same kind." The woman decided that the insole was not necessary, and limped out. . . .

What ever brought Hennessy into a department store will always be a mystery, probably; but there he was — Hennessy, one hundred and ninety-five pounds of plumber and gas-fitter! He wandered down the aisle in a befuddled sort of way, with the air of a man seeking nothing in the world but an exit. As he passed Mame's counter, whether it was her big mop of bronze hair or the red neckties with nice gold stripes in them that caught his eye, I cannot say. But the fact is, he hesitated; and you know what happens to the man that hesitates! And Mame had a very friendly face.

" O you!" cooed Hennessy as he came to the counter.

" G'wan," said Mame, coquettishly, " the kiddin' room is on the roof! Take the elevator an' get the air!"

" I was up there," said Hennessy, " but they told me you was down here. What might them be?" said he as he pretended to examine one of the gorgeous ties.

" Them is neckware," said Mame. " Fifty

cents to you, but half a dollar to anyone else. You better take a green one!"

" What you say goes wit' me," said Hennessy, " an' 't is me own choice besides. Do you kape collars?"

" We do not — we sell 'em," said Mame. " Do you want a nice, thick, leather one with brass nails in it — or mebbe you're shoppin' for somebody else an' want the linen ones?" and she took down several boxes. " You're lookin' in the wrong place — I ain't got 'em in my hair, they're on the counter here! Besides, the floor-walker is watchin' you — the store has lost a lot lately through shop-liftin'."

Hennessy grinned, and eyed the Earle Williams person contemptuously — " Him and me 'll go to the mat, if he butts in on me an' you, Kid. Lave me see them seventeen and a halfs.

For half an hour, Hennessy and Mame exchanged shots across the counter, and Hennessy bought a great many things he didn't want (even as you and I). And when he went, Sadie and Mazie and Lizzie and Genevieve and the rest descended on the flushed and happy Mame. " Who 's the John, Mame?" they chorused. " He certainly did camp here! He never seen nothing he bought, neither, for he never took his lamps off 'n yuh!"

" Ain't he a scream!" said Mame. " An'

say! He's no John, not by no means, he ain't. His name's Hennessy, an' he's a single party, an' him an' me's goin' to the Bricklayers' an' Mortar-Workers' Ball tomorrow night! Oh Boy! I knowed him for a regular guy the minute I lamped him!''

'' Five cents fine apiece for talking,'' said the floor-walker person, as the girls scattered at his approach.

'' I should worry!'' said Mame.

Sadie sat on the front steps of the rooming-house, the following evening, and watched Mame sail away on the arm of the stalwart Hennessy for the Bricklayers' Ball, and Sadie was heavy of heart. '' See that you come home sober, Mame!'' she called after them in a feeble attempt at raillery.

'' It's better to be brought home in ' the wagon ' than not to go!'' laughed the sharp-witted Mame; and such a rejoinder from one's pal doesn't exactly add to the gaiety of nations.

Sadie sighed, and studied the toes of her shoes. When she looked up, there stood Hooligan, the iceman, at the railing. There was that in his manner that was tentative. He had worshipped Sadie from afar for a good while, and had exchanged bits of repartee with her from the sidewalk mornings; but this was his first real tete-à-tete.

" For where is them two headed, wid all that
park harness on 'em, Miss Sadie? " he ventured.

" To the Bricklayers' Ball," said Sadie, " an'
I wisht I was, too! " said Sadie, — " not that
I'm hintin'."

" I hear from Casey 'twill be some party! "
said Hooligan. " He said he was pretty tired to
go, but he thought a couple o' fights would rest
'im. All guns an' brass knuckles checked at the
dure, an' every thing nice an' safe. Now,
if —— "

" You're on! " said Sadie, as she flew into
the house to dress.

It was a " regular " ball, although there were
really very few ambulance calls, and the reserves
came in only toward the end. Hooligan knew
almost everybody, and so did Hennessy, though
they didn't know each other; and when in the
mazes of a fox trot, Hooligan and Sadie bumped
violently into Hennessy and Mame, the two gentlemen immediately assumed belligerent attitudes
and started to remove their coats — which was
contrary to the injunction promulgated by a conspicuous sign reading, " *Gents Must Not Remove
Their Coats.* " And their perfectly evident intention to engage in battle was also contrary to the
rule laid down by another sign which read, "*Be
Nice! If You Want to Fight, Go to—Belgium!*"

Hostilities were averted, however, when the girls embraced, glad to see each other.

After the formalities of introduction had been concluded, the quartette adjourned to a table, presided over by a waiter who smoked incessantly; and who, in addition to serving drinks, was expected to sing, play the piano, eject undesirables, and keep an eye out for " dips." He was busy, at times.

" Honest, Mame," said the generous Sadie, as she looked over the top of her stein, " you certainly look grand tonight! That bunch o' hicks over there is rubberin' at you good an' plenty."

" I ain't got nothing on you, Sade; you're all to the Lady Duff-Gordon yourself! " replied Mame. All was peace. Hennessy inquired solicitously of Hooligan about the ice business; and Hooligan, in turn, asked quite as solicitously of Hennessy about the plumbing business. And each strove in genuine rivalry to " buy " oftener than the other. The ladies were a bit startled at a commotion in another part of the hall; but the waiter said, out of the corner of his mouth, " Keep your seats, ladies! No fire! That's just McManus beatin' up a Kike who was givin' three cheers for Ireland. What t'ell right has them Kikes got to cheer for Ireland? " And thus, it was a nice, cozy, comfortable little party; all correctness and amity — mostly.

Of course, when Maggie Grabbenheimer, the " perfect thirty-six " in " the gowns," came to the table and tried to horn in on the party, and Mame jostled a waiter who was bearing aloft a three-foot tray filled with ales, wines, liquors, and cigars, most of which went into the lap of Miss Grabbenheimer's new silk taffeta (1.69 a yard, reduced) there was some confusion, not unmixed with acrimony. But as Miss Grabbenheimer was " withdrawn " from the party before the commission of any overt act, things resumed their former placidity.

Hennessy wanted one more dance — " Let me give you another twist, Kid. The blood is all mopped up by now. I don't know them fox trot steps any too good, but this here's a waltz."

" Sure," said Mame, " I noticed you ain't. For such a big man, you're very light on my feet! " And off they went.

Hooligan, in the grip of his new patent leathers, looked appealingly at Sadie.

" Naw! " said the tactful Sadie, " I'd rather set it out — with you." And Hooligan had never heard any sweeter music than those words.

It was only a moment after the reserves broke in that the ladies decided it was time to be going home. Both Hennessy and Hooligan were rather reluctant — it seemed highly probable

that an opportunity would present itself to soak
a policeman or two — but both gentlemen gallantly denied themselves that pleasure, at the
request of the yawning ladies. At the door of
the rooming-house, Mame and Sadie assured
them that they had had " one grand time."

" The pleasure was all our'n," said the Ches-
terfieldian Hennessy.

" Thanks," said Mame. " Me for the Ostermoor. So long! "

At the corner, Hennessy and Hooligan shook
hands, at parting. " Say," said Hooligan,
" you're mebbe up in them kind o' things — how
much does a man have to pay down whin he
uys furniture for a little flat, d'ye know? "

" I do not," said Hennessy, " but I was
thinkin' of findin' out tomorrow, meself." And
then, as by mutual, telepathic consent, they
looked around the four corners to see if any
place was open wherein " men may put their
feet upon the brass rail, and deal with such
matters as they should be dealt with."

It was but a few weeks thereafter, that Hennessy stood upon the steps of the rooming-house,
late one night, and " put his fortune to the
touch."

" I got the furniture bought, and here's the
weddin' ring; I got a steady job, an' the boss

raised me today to thirty-five dollars a week. Would ye be knowin' aany gurl who'd marry me? " Mame had one hand on the door knob, and Hennessy had firm possession of the other. Sadie was listening at the window above.

Mame looked long into Hennessy's eyes. " Mike," she said, " gimme that ring quick, an' don't talk so loud or some of them Fifth Avenue fortune-huntresses will hear you, an' get it away from me! Thirty-five dollars a week! Mike, I didn't think Rockefeller got that much! But, listen, man, honest to Gawd, I'd take a chance with you if we have to live on my six! That's how much I know a girl that'll marry you! "

And as Mame's arm went about Hennessy's neck, Sadie drew her head inside the window, like the lady she was. " Ah, Hennessy," she sighed, musingly, " you don't half know what a lucky mug you are! "

And thus it was, that one Mike Hennessy " broke a pair of queens," as the saying is; or, rather, perhaps I should say he " drew one," and it strengthened his hand sufficiently to enable him to open the jack-pot of Matrimony. And in due time, he and Mame settled down to the joys of life (forget the ills — they don't count, anyway) in a Harlem flat; and Sadie was left in maidenly solitude in the little third-floor-front. But it must not be supposed that Sadie

Vitagraph *From "A Pair of Queens"—Featuring Flora Finch, Kate Price, Hughey Mack, and William Shea*

was going to be put into the discard. She was
still a " queen," even if she still toiled in " The
Ladies' Shoes."

Of course, Mame couldn't overlook a bet like
going down to Pimpel's and having Sadie try to
" fit her to a pair of shoes." After Sadie had
pulled down upwards of seventy-five pairs, none
of which suited, she said to Mame, " Mebbe you
better try in the men's department — they don't
come no larger here. Who is that talkin' to your
husband at the door? " Mame stifled the " hot
come-back " about the " men's department "
that she had on the tip of her tongue, and looked.
It was Maggie Grabbenheimer, " the perfect
thirty-six " in " The Ladies' Gowns." Mame left
hurriedly — so did Maggie Grabbenheimer, when
she saw Mame.

As may be surmised, Sadie did not remain
long in " The Ladies' Shoes." Hooligan bore
her off in triumph as his bride. Hennessy asked
him about it one day, for Hooligan's extreme
bashfulness was proverbial. " How did ye ever
have the nerve? " asked Hennessy.

" ' Nerve ' is right," said Hooligan. " 'Tis a
ticklish business askin' a foine gurl like Sadie
to marry the loikes o' me; but I wint at it foxy
like, an' overcome her objections be strategy. I
says to her wan evenin', ' would she go to the
movin' pitchers,' and she says ' would she! '

We walked up Six't' Aven'y an' she looks into a jewelry windy. ' Which av them rings would ye be likin' best? ' says I. ' Them plain gold wans,' says she; an' I thinks to meself what a sinsible gurl she is to prefer the plain wans to one wit' a rock in it. We passed several movin' pitcher places, but it seems she didn't like the bill. We come to wan wit' a weddin' it in. ' We'll go in here,' says she. ' Weddin's is my dish.' ' Ah ha! ' thinks I, ' mebbe there'll be somethin' in the pitcher that'll give me kind av an openin'.' It seems that in the pitcher there was a smooth guy had somethin' on the hick that was gettin' married to the gurl, an' he put the whole thing on the fritz. ' Ain't he grand? ' says she. ' I could bate the face off'n 'im,' says I. ' For why? ' says she. ' Fer crabbin' the weddin',' says I. ' He ain't the only wan that's crabbin' a weddin',' says she, lookin' at me funny like. ' I don't get ye,' says I. ' I didn't think ye would,' says she, not explainin'. While I was thinkin' this over, they changes the fillum. ' Do ye like Charley Chaplin? ' says I, seein' it was him comin'. ' I like the other kind better than Charley,' says she, laughin'. ' What other kind? ' says I. ' Do you mean his brother? ' She give me a long look. ' I didn't know he had wan,' says she. ' Oh, yes,' says I. ' He's very funny, too! ' ' There's those that's funnier than ayther av them,' says she, ' an' thicker, but they don't draw down no salary fer it.' I had a feelin' that I was out over me head, and wasn't makin' no progress wit' her; an' I set still watchin' the pitcher fer an openin' an' thinkin'. But none come, an' I was that discouraged. Whin we got home on the steps, — she never said nothin' all the way — she kind o' sighed like, an' says, ' 'T is turrible lonesome I am since Mame got married, an' me livin' all alone.' An' I says, ' Why don't ye have wan av the gurls at the store come an' room wit ye?' I says. An' wit' that, she fetches me a wallop in the brains that made me dizzy, an' I clinched wit' her till me head cleared. An' whin the sidewalk stopped spinnin', there I was wit' me arms around her, an' she a-cryin' agin' me shirt-front! An' me that embarrassed at the bouldness of me standin' there wit' me arms round her! Ye see, I was only clinchin' to kape her from landin' the right agin, an' meanin' nothin' wrong! But bein' in that position, mebbe the wallop give me nerve, mebbe, an' I says to her, — I says —— "

" Never mind what it was you says," said Hennessy, " ain't you the naughty thing, you audacious Dan Jewan, you! Young Lochinvar had nothin' on you! 'T is a gift to have nerve loike that wit' wimmen! "

And it wasn't long before Sadie and Aloyisius

came to live in the same Harlem flat, just underneath Mike and Mame; where confidences could
be exchanged down the dumb-waiter, and the
clothes hung out on the same roof. Where the
two families could sit on the front steps, on fine
evenings, in various stages of déshabillé, and
take turns going with the can over to "the
Dutchman's."

And O, Retributive Justice!—"Who do ye
think moved into the flat today?" said Mame,
as they all sat there one evening. "Was it
T'edore Rosenfelt, I dunno?" said Hennessy,
indifferently.

"Like 't was Willum Jennings Bryant,
mebbe?" said Hooligan between puffs of his
pipe, as he reached for the empty can.

"Nayther av 'em—bad luck to ye! ye have
me talkin' like ye!" said Mame. "'T was none
other than that Francis X. Williams guy down
at the store! He fell fer that little Mazie girl
in ' The Ladies' Hose.' The same dude that
used to fine us every time he looked at us!"

Hooligan and Hennessy sat up as one man,
and started to roll up their sleeves. "What
flure?" said Hennessy.

INDISCRETION

Produced by The Vitagraph Company of America.

Featuring LILLIAN WALKER.

Directed by Wilfrid North.

Old Marcellus Holloway had been a widower for more than fifteen years. A man of great wealth, he had buried himself among his books in his great library, taking little heed of other things, and had allowed his only child, Penelope, to bring herself up. Taking it " by and large," Penelope had made a very fair job of it, and at eighteen, she was lithe and strong and beautiful. Her horizon had been bounded by her father's vast estate and the countryside about it, through which she rode her horses and drove her automobiles, often to the consternation of the inhabitants. Her intimates, outside of her father, were horses and dogs and the books that her unrestrained and undirected fancy chose.

It cannot be said that the books were always those which a careful mentor would have selected for her, and there were wide gaps in her education. She had read much of history and mythology and the romances, and had puzzled her head over some philosophy and "advanced thought" and Socialistic doctrine; but she had never read a "best seller."

And if you had asked her, she probably would have told you that Brooklyn was the capital of St. Louis, and that she hadn't any idea at all what ½ of ¾ of 16 was. It was inevitable, under conditions like these, that Penelope grew up exceedingly courageous and self-reliant, and also self-willed and independent, and with an utter disregard for the restraints of convention.

The one intimate friend of the family was old Dr. McIntosh, a fussy, explosive, irascible, kind-hearted Scotchman, who had been the village physician for more than forty years, and who had been present at the birth of almost everybody in the village, including Penelope; and who dropped in almost daily to scold Holloway about his sedentary life among his books, and, incidentally, to have a "drop of Scotch" and a pipe while he was doing it.

He drove up to the door in his ramshackle buggy, alighted, leaving the ancient horse to his own devices, and bustled into the library. He found Holloway, as usual, poring over several books at once; and before he took the cordially

proffered hand, he sniffed the air disgustedly
and opened all the windows, allowing the entering breeze to blow Holloway's papers to all corners of the room. Then he proceeded to the
lecture, shaking a warning finger at Holloway,
who interrupted to call the Doctor's attention to
the fact that the butler was waiting. The Doctor looked at the butler and smiled. The old
butler also smiled, and went out, soon returning
with a tray filled with glasses and " the ingre-
dients," and the two old men settled back over
their toddy for a comfortable talk.

Penelope came into the stable-yard riding upon
one of the horses that drew the farm wagon,
holding a kicking rabbit by the ears. She slid
off the horse and held the rabbit high out of the
reach of several of the dogs that leaped for it;
finally beating them off, and handing the rabbit
to a groom, when she saw that the Doctor's
" rig " was at the door. She opened the door
of the library and came in softly and unnoticed
by the Doctor, just as he was telling Holloway
that he must get out of doors, pounding his own
rugged chest as an example, and making Holloway stick out his tongue. Then he saw Penelope, who ran to him and kissed him, to his great
satisfaction, and sat on the arm of his chair,
while he pointed to her as another example of
outdoor life. Then he made Penelope stick out

her tongue, as an exhibit of her health, and said it was a very good tongue indeed.

Penelope took a sip from her father's glass, and the Doctor had a fit about it, saying that it wasn't a thing that young girls should do. And though she didn't like the taste of it, the Doctor couldn't convince her that there was anything really wrong about it for her, if it wasn't wrong for him. So, after a good deal of bluster, the Doctor said he must be going, again telling Holloway that he must get out of doors.

The next day, Penelope took matters in her own hands and came into the library with two fishing rods and the appropriate paraphernalia, and insisted that her father follow the Doctor's orders and go fishing with her. He tried vainly to beg off, but she was insistent; and with a sigh of resignation, he tucked a big book under his arm and started. Penelope promptly took the book away from him; but he slyly put a smaller one into his pocket, and they went. As they went through the woods, Penelope managed to pick his pocket of the book, and it wasn't until he put a stone on his pole and then sat down on the stone, Penelope having gone further up the stream, that he felt for the book and smiled as he found it gone.

Penelope had trouble with her line, and promptly took off her shoes and stockings and

Vitagraph

Lillian Walker and Walter McGrail in "Indiscretion"

waded in to free it, and when she came back to her father, there was a fish on his hook making quite a fuss in the water, to which Holloway was blissfully unconscious, being deep in a calculation upon some notes he had in his pocket. Penelope landed the fish, and stood bare-footed as she told him what a poor fisherman he was.

Just then, the Reverend Mr. Peabody, the pastor of the village church, came upon them, in the midst of his quiet and meditative walk. He looked at the pair and mildly inquired if they had forgotten that today was Sunday. Holloway was greatly disturbed, and insisted that they had forgotten and that they would walk back with the parson. And down the highway they went, the bare-footed Penelope trudging along behind, still carrying the fish, and making faces at the parson, thus affording the passers-by another excellent opportunity to say something else about " that Holloway girl."

That night, on the piazza, Penelope thought a long time; then she said, " Daddy, is there anything really wrong about catching a fish on Sunday? "

Holloway squirmed a little, and then said, " I don't know that there is anything really very wicked about it, but people don't do it — it isn't quite — er — conventional, to say the least."

When he went in to the library, Penelope was still thinking about it with troubled face.

The village " censors " had decided that Penelope must be conventionalized. Meeting one day on the street, Miss Perkins and Miss Brown and Mrs. Higbee held a " panning bee." Miss Perkins told of Penelope's shameless fishing expedition of the past Sunday; and Mrs. Higbee told how her own husband, Hiram Higbee, had been at the " depot " to meet three friends with his Ford, and just as they started toward home, Penelope came running up and calling, " Hey, Hiram, gimme a lift to the house! "

" An' the brazen hussy jumped right onto the runnin' board and talked to Hiram an' them three other men! An' Hiram somehow got kind o' mixed up, not payin' attention to the car, for some reason or other, an' run plum into a fence and busted the machine, that he'd had only four years, all to flinders! "

The other women said " Land sakes! " And as Mr. Peabody and his wife came along at that moment, Miss Brown spoke right out and said that " such doin's was a positive scandal to the village, and she guessed that Mr. an' Mis' Peabody was the ones to see the hussy's father and see if she couldn't be made to act like other folks."

The parson and his wife didn't care especially for the job, but there seemed no way out of it; and so, later, they stood at the door of the Holloway house, and looked at each other, wondering what they were going to say. Mr. Holloway received them courteously, for he knew their intentions were good; and after they had opened up the subject, he sent the butler for Penelope. She was just mounting her horse, and came reluctantly into the library, clad in a tight fitting riding suit that showed off her figure to advantage. Mrs. Peabody gasped a little when she saw it, but being partly human, she wasn't really much pained or horrified. Penelope looked from one to the other, as though inquiring what it was all about; and just as her father was clearing his throat to begin, she saw the groom jerking the bridle of her horse impatiently. Penelope vaulted out of the low window and gave the groom a lecture on how not to handle horses. And then, even while the Peabodys looked from the window in approbation of what she had done, she mounted her horse and galloped away. Holloway looked at the Peabodys in a helpless, " what-can-you-do-with-a-girl-like-that " manner. Mrs. Peabody and her husband laughed, and suggested that it might be better to have Penelope accompanied on her rides about the country by a groom, or somebody; it was safer and more

conventional. And that it might be well to send
Penelope to a good school, "where she would
associate only with refined girls of the best
families."

To all of these things Mr. Holloway gave heed,
and said he would see what could be done. In
pursuance of this promise, Mrs. Travers, who
lived within motoring distance of the Holloway
home, in due time got a letter from Marcellus
Holloway asking that she run down for the week
end for a consultation, as she had been an old
friend of Penelope's mother, and had a daughter
herself. Mrs. Travers called together Jimmy,
her son, who was a lawyer, and a rather grave
and correct young man, and her daughter Margery. She showed them the letter, and Jimmy
offered to drive her to the Holloways the following day.

When Penelope started on her afternoon ride,
a groom accompanied her.

"What's this?" asked she.

"Mr. Holloway's orders, Miss," said the
groom.

"Nothing doing," said Penelope.

But her father appeared on the scene and
insisted, and Penelope and the groom started
away together, though there was a look on Penelope's face that didn't make the groom feel any
too comfortable. At the top of a steep embank-

ment over the lake, Penelope, who was walking
and leading her horse, dropped her hankerchief;
and as the groom stooped to pick it up, she gave
him a vigorous shove with her foot that sent him
rolling to the bottom and into the lake. Then
Penelope hit his horse a cut, and mounting her
own, rode away laughing — and to all of this,
Mrs. Travers and Jimmy had been witnesses as
he brought the car to a halt to inquire the way.

The groom scrambled up the bank, and to their
inquiry, told them that the Holloway place was
about a mile beyond, and that it was Miss Holloway who had just ridden away.

Mrs. Travers and Jimmy were about equally
interested, but for different reasons. They
looked at each other, and Jimmy sent the car
along, and the groom began a chase for his horse.

In the library, Mrs. Travers and Mr. Holloway
talked, and Jimmy was absent-mindedly looking
out of the window. He had had a glimpse of
Penelope, and he very much wanted another.
She came, finally, and in a moment, she and
Jimmy were deep in conversation, a little apart
from the others. Finally, Penelope took him by
the hand and led him out into the grounds. So
that by the time it was decided that Penelope
should go to a very select school with Margery
Travers, and they looked around to ask her how

she liked the arrangement, neither Penelope nor
Jimmy was in sight.

In the next three days, Penelope and Jimmy
had what she described as a " ripping " time;
and when it came time to go, she went up to
Jimmy and put her arm about his shoulder in
a most " pally " way, and suggested that Jimmy
stay that the good time might continue! The
situation was relieved by everybody, including
the old and privileged butler, laughing; and
Jimmy disengaged himself as gracefully as he
could, and drove away with his mother, leaving
Penelope waving from the piazza, and genuinely
sorry that he was gone. " Unconventional is
putting it mildly," thought Mrs. Travers.

And so, in due time, the two girls, Penelope
and Margery, were installed as room-mates at
Briarwood School, and took up their duties and
routine.

Of course, Penelope got into all kinds of
trouble by her ingenuous unconventionality.
Almost the first day, when the girls, a teacher
at their head, took their two-by-two walk in the
town, Penelope saw a young man having trouble
with his car, seemingly unable to fix it. She left
the file of girls, unobserved by the teacher, and
in a few moments, she had the engine going, and
had accepted an invitation from the young man

to drive her back to the school. As she drove
past the file of girls, the teacher saw her, and
there was a great time over it; but as usual,
Penelope couldn't see that she had done anything actually wrong.

"Perhaps," said the principal, "there is
nothing inherently wrong or wicked in what you
did; but society makes certain rules, called
conventions, which apply chiefly to women, and
those who disregard those conventions, suffer in
the opinion of society."

A few evenings afterward, "the refined girls
from the best families" gave Penelope and Margery a "house-warming" at midnight, with
chafing-dish and cigarettes. The principal
dropped in, unexpected and uninvited. And
all the girls but Penelope threw away their
cigarettes cleverly. Penelope stuck to her's.
She couldn't see why, if her father could smoke
all day long, there was anything wrong about it.
Then there was more advice about conventions.
Penelope's attitude was not one of impudent
defiance of rules; there was a genuine frankness
about it all that gave weight to her contentions,
sophistical though they were, and she was not by
any means in disfavor.

Then came the blow. Penelope was at basket-
ball on the campus, when the principal came
with the yellow envelope. In it was a message

from Duncan McIntosh, which said that her father was very seriously ill and that she must come at once.

The home-coming was a sad one. The old Doctor met her on the step, and took her into his arms, and she read the news in his face. She tore herself away and rushed into the darkened room and flung herself on her knees at the bedside of the dead man. The old butler and the Doctor came softly in and stood by her as she sobbed on her father's breast; then, brushing the tears from their own eyes, they went softly out again. . . .

For almost a year, Penelope hid herself from her friends, refusing to return to the school, and seeing no one but the old Doctor, who was now her guardian. Even Mrs. Travers and Margery, who drove down to see her, were refused admittance, and went away, after seeing Dr. McIntosh; not at all angry, but sorry for the poor, lonesome little soul that was grieving her heart out in the big library.

They went home and told Jimmy Travers all about it; and Jimmy resolved to do a little rescuing on his own account.

She was in the library pouring over " The Equality of the Sexes " and " Advanced Thought for Women " and such.

" Ye must get away from such books as

these," the old Doctor had said. "They're all written by long-haired men and short-haired women, and they're not for right-livin' folk. Why don't ye go visit Mrs. Travers, now?"

But Penelope shook her head, and the Doctor went away shaking his, too.

Jimmy came to the front door and presented his card. The old butler told him it was very doubtful if Penelope would see him, but that he would present the card. Jimmy slipped around to the side of the house and looked into the library window. Penelope stood with his card in her hand and there was a smile on her face as she pondered. Then she shook her head to the butler, but Jimmy jumped in by way of the window, and she was so glad to see him that she kissed him!

The Doctor dropped in shortly afterward, and the butler told him with gladness in his voice, that Penelope and Jimmy were out in the grounds, and the Doctor said, "God be praised!" He strolled out to find them and came upon them deeply interested in each other. Jimmy told him that he had come to invite her down to visit his mother and the Doctor urged her to go. She was reluctant and offered as a substitute motion—"I have it! Instead of my visiting Jimmy's mother, why can't Jimmy stay here with me?"

" May the good Lord give ye sense," said the Doctor. " I came to see ye on business — ye have so much money 'tis sinful — but I'm afeart yer advice wouldn't be worth much. Pack up and go and stay with Jimmy's mother for a while — 't is a mother yer needin'."

And so it was settled, and Penelope took up life among new surroundings and new faces in the Travers home. Of course, they brought her out of herself. Of course, there were new gowns and fixings, and of course there was a coming-out party.

To this party, Mr. and Mrs. Reginald Rivers were invited and they accepted. To be frank, Mr. and Mrs. Reginald Rivers got along about like two cats drowning in a bag, hating each other with great cordiality. The main cause of this discord was the conduct of Mr. Rivers toward other women. He was a shameless roué, and everything was fish that came to his net.

And the minute he laid his eyes on Penelope, he broke the tenth commandment into little bits (and laid deep and crafty plans as to how he could break — others). In a few minutes, he had appropriated Penelope, and he bore her off under the very noses of Jimmy and Mrs. Rivers. Soon they were talking books in a secluded nook in the conservatory, and he was agreeing heartily with her when she said that women were too closely bound by conventions and should have more freedom of action. Jimmy came and asked for a dance, and Penelope refused, saying she was too much interested in the book-talk; and Mr. Rivers uncovered a sneering smile at Jimmy's discomfiture.

Mrs. Rivers wasn't any too pleased, either; for though she hated her husband, she didn't care for that kind of humiliation before her friends and neighbors. And more than once, Jimmy and Mrs. Rivers bumped into each other as they moved among the dancers, and tried to keep an eye on the couple in the nook.

Rivers monopolized Penelope during the evening; and going home in the cab, he got as fine a little laying-out from his wife as falls to the lot of most men. But he only laughed at her, and this didn't make her feel any better about the matter. And when he went up the stairs, she stood in the library a long time, tapping her foot and biting her lip, — which actions, keen observers say, are sure danger signals.

Jimmy, when the guests had all gone, detained Penelope at the foot of the stairs, and made her a proposal of marriage — flat. Penelope was astonished, and was inclined to take the matter as a joke. She jerked her hand away and ran up the stairs, stopping half way to look back at him and laugh. Then she darted into her room and shut the door quickly, and stood with her back against it for a few moments, thinking hard, with heaving breast. Jimmy still stood at the foot of the stairs, shaking his head in perplexity.

This was only the beginning of Penelope's " scandalous " conduct with Rivers. She flirted openly with him at the golf club; and it wasn't long before the gossips got busy and whispered, " They say . . ."

Jimmy got so fussed, when she had a highball at Rivers' table on the piazza, that he went out and teed up a ball, took a wallop at it, missing it entirely, and smashing his driver into bits. He flung the fragments away, and went back to the club. On the way, he met Mrs. Rivers, and they joined forces. They went to the table and sat. Mrs. Rivers was inclined to be very " offish " with Penelope, but the girl's frank and ingenuous manner totally disarmed her, and she saw that the fault was, in all probability, her husband's, and that Penelope really thought nothing about how her intimacy with him looked. Jimmy sought to moralize with Penelope, and only succeeded in stirring up a fuss.

" Is it any crime to speak to a married man? " she said, when Jimmy told her that she must know that Rivers was married. And when they came into the hall, instead of stopping at the

foot of the stairs, Penelope marched straight up
to her room; and Jimmy went the other way,
sorry that he had said anything and more per-
plexed than ever. Penelope, in the conscious
rectitude of having done nothing wrong, couldn't
see why people should have such narrow views
about things which were really none of their
business.

Several evenings of foot-tapping and lip-bit-
ing had brought Mrs. Rivers to a determination.
She had an interview with a large and flat-
footed " gent," surnamed Harrigan, whose card
bore the legend " Private Detective. Evidence
obtained in divorce cases." And after a suitable fee had been accepted, Mr. Harrigan agreed
to keep an eye, or, in fact, several eyes, on Mr.
Rivers; and this he proceeded to do with efficiency. He planted two men in the golf club,
one as a waiter and the other as a playing guest,
having made a little private arrangement with
the steward — and Harrigan looked after matters on the outside.

At an " affair " at the club, one evening,
Rivers and Penelope left off dancing and came
to a table for refreshment. It was getting late
and many of the guests were leaving. Harrigan's man — the waiter — was serving.

Rivers said, so that the waiter could hear it,
though he didn't intend that he should, " We

are all going up to the road house for a little supper. Let us go ahead; the others will join us in a short time.'

Penelope demurred at first, but finally consented, and by the time Rivers had adjusted her wraps, and had her in his car, the waiter, the playing guest, and Harrigan were hustling into another car to follow.

Jimmy, too, had seen them as they drove away, and not liking the looks of things, got his car and followed. They all would have been close behind Rivers and Penelope, but for the fact that Harrigan had engine trouble, and had to stop. Jimmy overtook the detectives, and they explained that they were following a couple that had just left the club, and asked if Jimmy would help them out. And as Jimmy was doing the self-same thing, he agreed, and they drove away together.

Rivers and Penelope alighted at the road house, and in a moment they were shown into a room. It didn't look much like a place where a party was going to have supper, and Penelope said so. Rivers laughed and took off the mask. He said that the party was going to consist of themselves only; and he attempted certain little familiarities with the now frightened girl.

She objected, strenuously.

" Oh come," said Rivers, " what makes you

so finicky tonight? Any girl that is as free and easy as you, needn't pretend innocence to me. Give me a kiss and don't make such a fuss!"

But Penelope did make quite a fuss, and in the struggle, her dress was torn from her shoulders, and Rivers choked her until she lost consciousness. Then he picked her up and carried her into the next room and laid her on the bed.

Just about this time, Harrigan and Jimmy and the others broke in, and there was apparently all the evidence that was necessary. The detectives took a good look at him and at her, and that ended their business there. But it didn't end Jimmy's. He lit into Mr. Rivers, and when he got through, there wasn't much left of the furniture, or of Mr. Rivers, either; and he was glad enough, when they had pried Jimmy loose from him, to sneak out of the room, and out of the story.

Penelope had recovered consciousness during the fight, and she watched the battle with agonized eyes. Too late, she had realized that Jimmy had spoken the truth when he had told her that " a woman must not only avoid doing evil, but she must avoid even the appearance of doing evil." When the fight was over, she ran to Jimmy and flung her arms about his neck and sobbed on his breast; but Jimmy was not at all responsive; he disengaged her arms gently, and then put her wraps over her, and led her from the house.

At the Travers home, Mrs. Travers and Margery were anxiously awaiting them, for they had got wind of the affair, though nothing definite. Jimmy came in, grim and silent, and the penitent Penelope followed after him. She rushed to Mrs. Travers to explain that she " had done nothing wrong," but that lady was decidedly chilly toward her, and Margery was summarily sent out. Jimmy started up the stairs; Penelope called after him appealingly; he stopped, looked at her for a moment, then turned and went on. Mrs. Travers asked one or two sharp questions, and then she, too, went out. And Penelope was left, leaning against the newel post, weeping and broken-hearted.

Of course, there was only one thing for Penelope to do — leave the Travers and go to her own home. Too late, she realized that the Walls of Convention have very valiant and watchful defenders.

Next day, she was all packed and ready to go, when the butler entered and said that a gentleman waited to see her in the hall; and she came down the stairs, dressed for traveling, and wondering who it could be. A man asked her if she was Miss Holloway, and on being informed that she was, handed her a formidable looking paper.

From "Indiscretion"—Featuring Lillian Walker

Jimmy, who happened to be crossing the hall, saw it and took it from her, and read it. She looked her inquiry, and he said, taking a long time about it, that it was a complaint in the action for divorce of Rivers vs. Rivers, and that Mrs. Rivers had named her, among several other women, as corespondent.

This was the last straw, and Mrs. Travers heard her pitiful cry of protest and came. Well Jimmy and his mother knew that this was unwarranted, and there came over them that revulsion of feeling, that reaction which we feel when we know that gross injustice is being done, even to one who is not entitled to our sympathy. And Mrs. Travers folded the poor motherless girl in her arms, took off her hat and coat, motioned to Jimmy to go away, and led Penelope up the stairs, telling her that they would stand by her to the last ditch in any such matter as that.

That night, while Jimmy studied late over the papers and formulated plans, Penelope stole out of the house and went straight to Mrs. Rivers. The butler told Penelope that Mrs. Rivers could not see her, but Penelope brushed by him and into the library, and the two women confronted each other. And then, Penelope told her simple story — the story of her bringing up; how her friends had always been men and dogs and books

— and of her escapade with Rivers. She didn't try to hide anything, or gloss it over, and she didn't grovel; but she did ask that Mrs. Rivers forego this hideous charge, in which there was no truth, and which would ruin her life.

And Mrs. Rivers knew that she had made a mistake. She took her back to the Travers home and delivered her. They had noted her absence, and Jimmy was about to start out to find her, fearing many things. In the hall, at the foot of the stair she and Jimmy stood again, for Mrs. Rivers and Mrs. Travers had moved away as they talked. Jimmy spoke to her, and there was something in his voice that made her drop her eyes, and she did not move. Jimmy spoke again and held out his arms, but she did not see them. Then he spoke sternly, and she lifted her eyes and they met his, and she came slowly to him, faltering.

" Jimmy," she said, " do you think it is quite proper for us to be here alone? You know I am going to be very careful about those things now."

THE PARSON OF PINE MOUNTAIN

Produced by The Universal Film Company.

Featuring BEN WILSON.

Directed by Ben Wilson.

With one powerful hand upon the plough and in the other an open bible, the Parson ran the furrow across the field, stopping at intervals, that he might better read and digest the pages, and incorporate their teachings in his sermon for the morrow. Down at the still, in the thick fastnesses of the mountain woods, Old Man Marvin and Steve Bascombe covered the fires, and leaving one of the others on guard, started home. As they passed the field where the Parson was ploughing, he hailed them and made them promise that they would come to meeting tomorrow. They made the promise without the least idea of keeping it, and under their outward deferential demeanor, it was plain that there lay a sort of inherent contempt for this man of peace. And as they went, Steve, a young giant of the mountains, looked laughingly back at the

Parson, with a derision that seemed almost a challenge.

Before the Marvin cabin, Lissy talked to two of the girls of the neighborhood, who, barefooted and ragged as she, had pails of blueberries on their arms. Old Man Marvin went into the house with only the curt greeting customary in the mountains; but Steve stopped to talk with the girls, though it was patent that he had eyes for no one but Lissy. And she, knowing this full well, teased him accordingly. She took some blueberries in her white fingers and holding them in front of his face, made him " open his mouth and shut his eyes." And while he stood there in that manner, she ate the blueberries herself. When Steve realized the trick, he caught her and kissed her forcibly, and went down the road laughing at her. Lissy pretended to be terribly angry and wiped her mouth with her hand; but as the girls left, she was still looking after Steve, and her face was smiling.

On Sunday morning, the Parson came from his cabin, bible in hand, clothed in the garb of the mountain preacher, and started for the outdoor meeting. Lissy made her father wash his hands and face at the basin on the bench outside the door, and go with her, though he didn't really want to. Steve hitched up his " horse and buggy," and as he drove over the rough mountain road he had trouble with the horse; and by the time he overtook the Parson, both he and the horse were in bad temper. Steve lashed the animal, and then jumping from the buggy, he was about to administer a most cruel beating to it, when the Parson stayed his hand. Steve turned fiercely upon him; "what business was it of his what he did to his horse?" and he brought down the whip with a swish over the Parson's shoulders.

The Parson didn't move, and again Steve lashed him for a meddler, contemptuous of the man that would take a blow unresented. The Parson opened his bible evidently intending to read a passage to Steve in regard to his conduct, when Steve knocked the book from his hands into the dust of the road.

And right there, Steve got one of the greatest surprises of his young life; for the Parson leaped upon him and gave him as artistic a trimming as ever a young hot-head got. When it was all over, he told Steve to pick up the book. Steve did it, but with an ill grace. The Parson sat Steve down by the roadside and opened the book to read to him.

"You all had no call to disrespect the bible thataway, Steve," he said. "That's what I had to lick you for. Now you set there and listen to

what it says about a man's bein' merciful to
dumb critters.''

And Steve had to hear it, too, though the Parson was obliged to knock him down again before
he was really willing to listen. And then he sat
down beside the battered Steve, put his arm
about his shoulders, and talked like a father to
him. And in the end, he and Steve shook hands
and went down the road to the buggy together,
got in and rode to meeting.

In the open glade, to the few people of the
mountains, the Parson preached his homely sermon, and made his earnest prayer. Lissy sang,
and as she finished, there were two who had not
taken their eyes from her — they were Steve and
the Parson. But after the meeting, Lissy got
into Steve's buggy and drove away, and the
Parson went home alone, thinking.

That night, the revenue men came to the still
and grievously wounded one of the band; he got
away, however, and was soon in the deep mountain fastnesses, cared for by his companions.
But they were not equal to the job. After a
conference, Steve, who was drinking heavily, was
called, and sent for Old Man Marvin and the
Parson — they had skill in such things.

And as it came about, Lissy was left alone
before the cabin in the moonlight, when the men
had gone. Steve turned back in the woods, tell-

ing Marvin and the Parson that he would take another way to reconnoiter. Lissy lighted the candle in the rough room of the cabin, when she heard a noise at the door; she saw that the hook was safe in the staple, but she was frightened. It was Steve, and he demanded to be let in. She refused. And then he put his powerful shoulder to the door, for he was deep in drink, and the staple flew from its hold, and as Steve stepped into the room, Lissy cowered before him.

On the way back, when they had ministered to the wounded man, almost at the door of Marvin's cabin, the Parson turned to the old man and said, " Mr. Marvin, I want to marry Lissy, if she'll have me. Do you all object? "

Marvin assured him that he did not in the least, and they entered the cabin door. Lissy sat at the table, her head bent upon her outstretched arms in the flickering light of the candle. The Parson went straight to her, and Marvin looked at the broken fastening of the door. The Parson took Lissy's hands and told her his love. She sank in a crumpled heap at his feet. The Parson looked from her to Marvin, and then to the open and broken door. The light was beginning to dawn upon him.

Old Man Marvin strode grimly over to the fireplace and took down his long rifle. But the Parson stayed him. Marvin tried to wrench away the gun, but he could not.

The Parson turned to the sobbing girl, " Lissy, do you love Steve Bascombe? " She at least did not deny it. The Parson nodded to Marvin, and went out, his face set hard. He caught Steve as he rode down the trail, with a few things that he had taken with him in his flight. He stopped the horse and Steve got off; he slapped the horse after turning it around, and it went back. He threw Steve's bundle into the brush at the roadside, and they went back together; not a word had been spoken. Just as they came to Marvin's, two of the mountaineers joined them, and Old Man Marvin came from the door and stood undecided and helpless.

Had it not been for the Parson's hand, he would have sprung at Steve's throat. The Parson smiled and said, " Lissy and Steve are aimin' to get married, and Steve come and got me. I'm kind o' standin' sponsor for Steve, too. He's made me a lot of promises about liquor and things, and he's goin' to keep 'em. Ain't you Steve? "

Steve went into the door; Lissy sat with drooped head. She raised her eyes to his, and he sprang toward her and took her into his arms. Outside the Parson moved a little away from the others; but as they called him, he steeled himself, took the worn bible from his pocket, and followed them in, pausing at the door to look back and to square his shoulders, as men do when they are brave and go to certain death.

UNCLE JOHN

Produced by The Universal Film Company.

Featuring Etienne Girardot.

Directed by Lucius Henderson.

It was pretty cold on the East Side; coat-collars were turned up, and noses were turned blue, but Jimmy Moore, age eight, found that getting enough money for supper for Alice and Pudge, who were waiting for him in the tenement, kept him warm. It is tough to have to assume the responsibilities of a family at the age of eight years, especially when one is a newsboy; but father Moore hadn't shown up for more than a week — it was probable that he was paying one of his periodical visits to The Island — and the three children were trying to keep the little home together. And Jenks, the agent for the landlord, would be there for the rent, and he had to be paid, too. So it was a case of " hustle " for Jimmy.

Old John Waldron, many times a millionaire, never had any patience with charity and settlement work; and when Horace, his only son, took it up with the fortune left him by his mother, the Old Man was disgusted.

" The Poor — Bosh! If a man is poor, it's his own fault. Let the poor work or starve! "

And Horace would say " No, it is work *and* starve with many of them. You are taking money which you don't need, for property that you never saw, from those who have to starve to give it to you."

These discussions got more and more acrimonious, until finally, one day, Waldron ordered his son out of the office. And Horace, with the impetuosity of youth, decided to leave home, too. And thus it was that John Waldron sat alone in his big library, brooding; and Horace settled down in a modest room, to help the poor.

Some days before, Horace had obtained permission from his father to collect the rents of one of his East Side tenements, that he might see Poverty at first hand. There he had met Helen — ("the nice girl across the hall who paints pictures," was the way the little Moores described her) and he had thought a great deal about her since. He concluded that one of the best ways to relieve poverty, was to encourage art. So he sent a friend to buy some of Helen's pictures, which Horace took off his hands, of course, "merely as a matter of philanthropy,"

Horace assured him. He also offered, by letter, to buy the tenement from his father.

The Old Man tore up the letter in a rage, and then made up his mind that he would go to see the tenement that was kicking up all this fuss. He had had two or three jars lately, and the thing got on his nerves. He went. As he entered, anybody who saw him would have concluded that he lived there. His clothes were the prevailing style for real millionaires; they can usually be purchased for about sixteen dollars, and are worn a long time.

He climbed the rickety stairs and looked all about him; nothing seemed very remarkable. On his way down, he didn't see the broken step, and he landed in the hall before the little Moores' door, with a badly sprained ankle, saving himself from breaking his neck only by hanging on to the banister.

The three little Moores heard the fall, and came out and found what looked to them like a poor old man in a peck of trouble. They helped him into their rooms; and after they had administered first aid to the injured and made him as comfortable as possible, they held a consultation. Here was a stranger within their gates and he surely needed some kind of medicine for that ankle, and he looked as though a little food wouldn't hurt him. Alice emptied the coffee-pot of its pennies, and Jimmy went out to get the stuff.

Waldron tried to hear what the conspiracy was all about, but couldn't quite get it. "We'll see what the Poor will do for the Rich," he said to himself.

Jimmy returned with a small package of tea, an orange, and a bottle of vile-smelling liniment. Jimmy treated his ankle, and Alice served the tea and the orange on a box which she placed beside the couch.

"Kindly little beggars," thought Waldron. He drank the tea and tried to share the orange; they would have none of it; it was all for him. And then Waldron asked when they were going to have their supper. Before Alice could stop her, the talkative Pudge said, cheerfully, "We ain't goin' to have any supper tonight, 'cause we spent all our money."

Waldron sat up straight and looked from one to the other as he realized their sacrifice. He tried to speak, but somehow he couldn't. And at that moment, in walked two officials of the "Gerry Society" without knocking and with an air of great authority. Deep in the heart of every East Side child is implanted a fear of "The Gerrys," and the children instinctively ran to Waldron, who sat very straight and stern, facing the two officials with a look on his face which, when railroad presidents saw it, made them go and put their property in their wives' names.

"To what do I owe this unwarranted intrusion?" said Waldron. "You should be prosecuted for disturbing my family — I — I am their uncle." And the two officials stood not on the order of their going. As the children drew a sigh of relief and clung closer to him, Waldron put his arms about them — actually he did!

That night, Waldron lay upon the rickety couch and pondered many things. He concluded that it might not be such a bad thing to stay a few days with the children, completely hidden from the cares of business, and study a little Sociology himself.

"If you haven't got any home," said Pudge, "why don't you stay with us, Uncle John?" And Waldron said that if he were to do that, he guessed it was about time to pay some board. They didn't want to take it, but he insisted; and after much whispering between Jimmy and Uncle John, the boy went out, and came in, staggering under the burden of good things. Uncle John boasted about what a good cook he was; so they put the big apron on him, and he folded a newspaper into a cook's cap, and got busy.

Jimmy ran across the hall and dragged " the nice girl " over to see him. (If only Wall Street could have seen him!)

Helen entered into the fun; she tasted Uncle John's cooking and pretended it made her sick; and Uncle John threatened her with a big spoon and got so excited that he let the toast burn. Pudge made him make some more.

About this time, Horace Waldron sat in his room, looking at the pictures which he had bought from Helen by proxy. But as he looked, always a vision came of her as he saw her first, sitting cross-legged, wrapped in her big coat, eating crackers and milk, and reading a book. (This is the orthodox picture of all poor but deserving lady artists.) And the more Horace thought about it, the more convinced he became that a few painting lessons would help him wonderfully in his work among the poor! He got his courage up and went to see Helen about it. The door was open and he went timidly in. Helen came back from the Moores to find him standing in admiration before her easel. After a good deal of hemming and hawing, the matter was arranged and Horace went to work at it, though he was always trying to draw pictures of Helen, who scolded him and tore up the pictures. But the entrée was established and he came regularly.

John Waldron was too big a man to drop out of sight for a week unnoticed, and one evening he read in the paper an account of his disappearance. He laughed. He laughed quite often now; formerly he had not laughed at all, except in derision. A knock came on the door; if he had disappeared, he might as well stay disappeared; so Waldron ducked into the inner room.

It was Jenks, the collector. Alice was a few cents " shy," and wanted Jenks to come back for it.

" No," said Jenks, " the old skin-flint who owns the building would fire me if he thought I would trust anyone for fifteen cents! I'll pay it myself."

Waldron, of course, heard it and was inclined to be angry at first; then he laughed, for he knew Jenks was right. And again listening through the same door, he heard Horace tell Helen that his father had disappeared, and that while he had parted from him in anger, he was very dear to him and that he would never be happy until he found him. And the whole matter came very near being adjusted there, only Horace left too quickly. For a certainty, John Waldron was getting humanized!

That night, Pudge had too much jam and the resultant " tummy-ache." Waldron got very worried about her, and started out for the doctor. An incoming " drunk " lit a cigarette in the hall and threw the blazing match into a pile of rubbish. When Waldron and the doctor got back, smoke poured in volumes from the entrance. He and the doctor plunged into the house, the doctor to come staggering out in a moment, blinded by the smoke. Waldron kept on; he got to the room and burst in the door. The children had fallen asleep when Pudge's ache had stopped, and were just wakening and groping in the smoke. Waldron wrapped some clothes about their heads, and sent Jimmy and Alice down the stairs. He picked up Pudge and started to follow, but the stairs to the floor above fell, blocking the door, and he went out of the window and down the fire-escape to the floor below, and was hopelessly blocked and hemmed in by the boxes and refuse which the East-Sider usually keeps there. As he stood for a moment irresolute, Horace and Helen, who were returning from the theatre, saw him.

" Oh! it is Uncle John," she screamed.

" It is my father! " gasped Horace, and he plunged into the building. He got to them none too soon, and fought his way down the blazing stairs with his double burden. . . .

Uncle John sat in the library, looking into the fire. Behind him, at the window, stood Horace and Helen, very close together, looking at some

pictures which seemed to interest Helen greatly.
They were those which she had sold to Horace's
friend, and the reason of her " big sale " was
apparent, and Horace's little scheme of philanthropy was revealed in all its shamelessness!
Blushes of confusion covered her cheeks, and
she did not dare look at Horace, though he was
looking very intently at her. In bounced Alice
and Jimmy, well dressed and with school books
in their hands. Pudge followed with a very big
piece of very sticky candy. They swarmed all
over Uncle John, and some of the candy got in
his whiskers, but he only laughed. Finally, the
observant Pudge called attention to Horace and
Helen — Uncle John had to turn clear around in
his chair to see them. Horace was holding Helen
very tight, and whispering to her. Uncle John
pretended that it was a great breach of etiquette
to look, and turned their heads away for them;
but they broke away and ran to Helen, who took
them into her arms.

Uncle John stood up and looked at his watch.
" Bless my soul! " he said, " I hadn't any idea
it was so late! Don't wait dinner for me —
maybe you won't miss me much tonight, anyhow. I 've got a long list of poor families that
I must see this afternoon, and then I'm going
to the architects to see about remodelling all
those tenements. So long! "

LUCIA

Produced under title, "The Tell-Tale Step."

Produced by Thomas A. Edison, Inc.

Featuring SHIRLEY MASON and
BOBBY HUGGINS.

Directed by Burton George.

Giovanni Pallazzi, with his arm about his blind daughter, stood at the rail of the steamer as it came slowly up the bay. As he passed the giant statue, he reverently doffed his hat; and as the beauty and grandeur of this Promised Land spread out before him, the emotional Italian painted for her ears the picture that was veiled from her sightless eyes. And when he stepped upon the pavement at the Battery, he knelt and kissed what seemed to him to be sacred ground; even as the Genoese had done, almost five hundred years before. And Lucia knelt beside him, her precious violin hugged close to her breast, and thanked God from the bottom of her pure little heart, that they were in the Land of Liberty.

For Giovanni had fled from the wrath of the Camorra, though Lucia didn't know it. But she did know that there were always troubles and something to fear at home, and she felt that those things were over now. Poor little thing! She did not know that the Camorra has a very long arm; but Giovanni knew it — and shuddered.

They took up abode in humble lodgings among their own people, and as they entered, the ragged Pietro, the much abused stepson of Luigi, sat upon the steps, whither he had fled to escape a beating from his stepfather, and looked with wide, brown eyes into Lucia's face — and from that time he was her devoted slave and shadow. The little family had found at least one friend in the New Land. Passionately fond of music, the boy would sit for hours at her feet while she drew the melody from the bosom of her violin; and at other times, he taught her as much of the strange language as he himself knew — a very willing and adoring master, and a very saucy and precocious pupil. They gave Pietro the freedom of their home, and he stole in and out and stayed or went, much as a cat would have done; and no dog ever had the blind, unreasoning devotion for his master that Pietro had for Lucia.

Beneath the junk shop of Luigi, which was more or less a " blind " for his real business, was a cellar, entered by a trap door concealed by a pile of old rugs and carpets. Here met a branch of the Camorra whose ban and sentence had fallen upon Giovanni at home; and here, in due time, came a letter which bade them, as loyal members, carry it out. Dimitri was selected, fôr he had known Giovanni in Italy, and he must find him here; and he took up the trail much as a hound takes up the scent.

He found Giovanni without much trouble, and one evening, as Lucia sat playing to Pietro and her father, she started — " Someone is at the door," she said. Giovanni and Pietro had heard nothing, but she insisted, and Giovanni went to the door and opened it. There, thrust into the outer door, was a stiletto, the death warning! Instantly, Giovanni held his finger on his lips and looked at Pietro, who nodded and understood.

Giovanni noiselessly took the stiletto from the door. " There is no one here, Little One," he said.

" There was," said Lucia, " I heard his step."

Giovanni and Pietro assured her that she must be mistaken, but though she said nothing, she was unconvinced. She had many times given evidence of the accuracy of her hearing, and would tell Pietro, as they sat together at " lessons," that her father was coming, although

Pietro could hear nothing; and she was always right.

Giovanni came in one evening; Lucia and Pietro sat together talking. He bolted the door and saw to the catch on the window — he was very careful these days — and sat in his chair. As the hour grew late, he nodded and finally slept. Pietro bade Lucia good-night and unbolted the door and went. Lucia slipped to her father's side, lightly kissed his hair and went into the inner room to bed.

Down the steps came the stealthy form of Dimitri and crept softly to the door. He turned the knob and opened it — his victim slept before him and he stepped into the room. Lucia, at her prayers, raised her head and listened; then started up and came into the room, calling " Father! " and as Dimitri darted out of the door, he saw the white figure in the doorway, but he knew that she could not see him, and that he was safe! Foolish Dimitri!

There was the usual long and vain investigation. The District Attorney, Hugh Graham, had suffered a nervous breakdown, and things dragged more than was customary. Lucia always told them that she had heard the man's step — he had been at the door once before, but her father and Pietro had tried to conceal it from her — and she could tell it among a million.

But that availed nothing — then. Luigi came with suave words and kindly acts, for he knew from Pietro about the wonderful girl.

And the agents of The Children's Society came too and were very officious. In every child of the East Side is an abiding terror of " The Society," and Pietro, while he feared that all would not be well with her if she went to Luigi's home, felt that it would be better than at " The Gerrys," and he advised her to go. And then Luigi showed the agents his home and said that he would treat her like one of the family — which was no lie. He did.

He had an awful time making her go out on to the street to play her violin for pennies, but he finally prevailed. He took the food from her plate and shoveled it onto his — " Those who eat must work," quoth he; and Pietro looking on helplessly, gripped the handle of his table-knife harder. Then he took away her beloved violin, and she sat for days, twisting her idle hands, until at last, she gave up. Rosetta, Luigi's wife, dressed her in picturesque rags, and Luigi put her violin in her hands with a sneering, triumphant smile, and with Pietro as her guide, he sent her out. As they were about to start, and it was very cold, he called Pietro back and cut and tore his shoes to ribbons and took away anything of warmth that the boy had upon him, that sympathy might be the greater.

The District Attorney sat in the big library of his sister's home, convalescing from the nervous breakdown. Mrs. Arbuthnot was most fond and proud of him, and most attentive. She had even picked out a wife for him in the person of Miss Stryver, a tall and beautiful girl, aristocratic, "with such an air about her," Mrs. Arbuthnot said.

And Miss Stryver "had ideas," too. She and Mrs. Arbuthnot were doing their best to entertain him and "keep his mind off things." Miss Stryver decided that he should be read to; and turning up her nose at anything in the well-filled bookcases, she took from her own handbag a volume marked "Mrs. Pankhurst's Speeches," and started in. Poor Graham could do nothing but grin and bear it.

And then, from beneath the window, came the wonderful strains of a violin. Graham heard it and brightened as he listened. Mrs. Arbuthnot and Miss Stryver were much annoyed, and were for ordering the butler to "shoo away" the street musician. But Graham refused to allow it; and when the music had ceased, he sent the butler out with a dollar bill. Miss Stryver resumed her reading. She rounded out a period,

Edison   From "The Tell-Tale Step"—Featuring Shirley Mason, Charles Sutton,
Pat O'Malley and Bobby Huggins

emphasizing it by walloping the book with her clenched fist, and said, "And Mrs. Pankhurst was right! Don't you think so, Mr. Graham?"

And Graham, opening his eyes, sat up quickly and said, "Yes, I think it was the most beautiful music I ever heard." And Miss Stryver's face would have made a grand little "still" for the exhibitor. So, during the long convalescence, Graham came to look for the two pitiful little figures that came beneath his window, and to enjoy, more and more, the music of the inspired violin.

One day, as she sat in the inner room, she heard *The Step* in the shop; Dimitri had come up from the cellar, where he had been pouring a bright metal into moulds that looked as though they ought to belong to Uncle Sam. She started toward the door, but Rosetta restrained her a moment, and Dimitri went out, unconscious of his danger. But Lucia knew that she had heard *the* man, and that in time, she would surely find him.

As Graham improved, they came to him from the office with business. An assistant and two Central Office detectives were with him on this occasion, and they were discussing the Pallazzi murder. "While a great many things point to this man Dimitri," said the assistant, "the case against him isn't at all strong, and we need some direct evidence connecting him with the murder.'' And while Graham was considering the matter, the music started in the street. They all listened, Graham standing by the window. When Lucia ceased playing, he took a bill from his pocket and threw it out. Pietro gathered it up, and sullenly doffed his ragged hat. The others came to the window and one of the detectives started. '' Why, that is the blind daughter of the murdered man, Pallazzi! '' he said.

While they watched, they saw Luigi come to the pair and roughly take the bill from Pietro and hurry them along to new pastures. '' Follow them,'' said Graham, and the detectives hurried out.

Toward night, weary and worn, and with the detectives still in their wake, Luigi and Lucia and Pietro came in front of Luigi's shop. As they were about to enter, they were met by two sleek, well-dressed young men, and a woman who was plainly of the underworld — way under. They spoke to Luigi a moment, and he called back Lucia, who came dejectedly. Pietro came, too, but a clout on the ear from one of the young men and another from Luigi, sent him reeling back.

The quartette looked Lucia over, appraisingly. '' Playing the fiddle is no business for her,''

they whispered into Luigi's receptive ear —
Luigi had been thinking that, himself. One of
the young men ventured a little familiarity with
Lucia, and got a wallop for his pains from her,
just forestalling Pietro, who was about to do
the same thing.

"Aha!" thought the "cadet." "Genuine
and worth having!"

And Luigi sent Lucia and Pietro into the shop,
and talked a while with the trio, who laughed
at him. Luigi entered and closed the door of
the shop and stood against it, thinking; Lucia
sat in the inner room and heard him coming.
Against the stone of the back step, Pietro sharpened and pointed the table knife. Luigi entered
and looked at Lucia; she felt his gaze and shrank.
He sent Rosetta out on an errand, and then he
crept toward the trembling girl, as Tarquin crept
upon Lucrece. Dimitri, in the cellar, was pouring metal into moulds. Lucia instinctively laid
down her violin and prepared for his approach.
He sprang upon her and wrapped his arms about
her. She beat at his face with her fists, and she
sunk her white teeth into his arm; but it would
have been of little avail, had not Pietro burst
in with his sharpened knife, and slashed mur-
derously at the man. Luigi let go long enough
for Lucia to wriggle from his grasp and to dart
to the shop and toward the outer door. Dimitri,

hearing the noise above, came from the cellar and started toward the door. She heard his step — *The Step* — and she grappled with him and screamed.

In the inner room, it would have been a duel to the death, but at the scream, the detectives broke into the front door and Luigi hurried to the shop, followed by Pietro.

"This is the man who killed my father!" she screamed. "This is the man!"

And when it was all over, the detectives led away Dimitri and Lucia to Headquarters, and Pietro followed.

They 'phoned to the District Attorney. "Bring her here and I will question her," he answered, "and my sister will take charge of her if you fear for her safety." And thus it was that Lucia became installed in the home of Mrs. Arbuthnot, until such time as the trial should be held.

Pietro got a fearful beating from Luigi after he had found him cowering on a doorstep and had dragged the boy home; probably he would have killed Pietro in his efforts to make him tell where Lucia was, had it not been for old Rosetta, who stayed his hand at last. But Pietro remained mute, and would not tell.

The gang, Dimitri's friends, demanded of Luigi that he find and dispose of the girl; he had let her escape, and she would be an important witness against Dimitri; and they gave him a week to do it in. And thereby, Luigi found himself very much up against it, and would go to any length to find her.

In Mrs. Arbuthnot's home, Lucia played her violin and became loved by everyone but Mrs. Arbuthnot and Miss Stryver. She grew to listen for Graham's step and to wait for his coming. Graham was unwilling to confine her in the House of Detention, and he was fearful for her safety if he let her go; so there she stayed. Pietro used to steal out nights and creep into the gardens about the house and whistle softly, and Lucia would hear him and come, and they would talk for a moment — the one bright spot in Pietro's life these days. But Luigi followed him, and as he took his evil face out of the shrubbery, he smiled and prepared.

Graham had spoken to Dr. Oppenheim, a noted eye specialist, about Lucia's eyes, and the old man agreed to come and look at them to see if anything could be done. The doctor found them all in the library, Lucia playing for them, while Mrs. Arbuthnot and Miss Stryver looked at her through their lorgnettes and said, "How interesting!" and "Very pretty, indeed." The old scientist examined Lucia's eyes, and said that he felt sure he could remove the difficulty. Miss

Stryver said, " How interesting! " and Mrs. Arbuthnot was about to tell the scientist " what a lovely time they had had at the Mothers' Meeting that day and how Miss Stryver had made a perfectly lovely talk on ' How to Bring Up Children,' " when Graham suggested that Lucia play for the old man. When she finished, the old man's face was buried on his breast, and a tear or two glistened in his whiskers. He got up and left, after reverently kissing Lucia on the forehead.

Graham sat with his head in his hand. Mrs. Arbuthnot and Miss Stryver had gone, long since. His fingers touched the doctor's instrument case, which the old man had forgotten. He looked at Lucia, and across his face there swept a wave of love and passion, and he started as though to take her into his arms. But instead, he called the maid, who led Lucia away to bed, and Graham sat long into the night, thinking.

Luigi and the gang pulled it off as per schedule. They followed Pietro in a car — it was a few days after the operation, and Oppenheim said that on no account must the bandages be removed in less than ten days. Pietro came into the gardens and whistled. The nurse had left the room, and Lucia was sitting in a big chair. She slipped out of the house in the night, and went to Pietro and told him all about it. One of the gang knocked Pietro on the head, and another put a handkerchief of chloroform to Lucia's face and a cloak over her, and they took her to the cellar, the existence of which no one outside of the gang, not even Pietro, knew. The two men left her with Luigi and Rosetta, and Luigi started to bind Lucia in a chair.

Graham, informed of Lucia's disappearance, found Pietro in the grounds, and when he recovered consciousness, they made all haste to Luigi's shop. It was locked. Pietro slid around and crept into the back window, while Graham summoned two policemen, and waited. Pietro upset a chair, and Luigi heard it and paused, with Lucia, half bound, and came up the ladder. In the shop, having no time to close the trap door, Luigi and Pietro faced each other, Pietro with his knife in his hand. In the cellar, Lucia struggled at her bonds and wriggled free, but Rosetta sought to hold her. In the strange place, Lucia tore off the bandage from her eyes, and *she could see!*

She fought off the aged Rosetta and sprang for the ladder, and got her hands on the ledge, when Rosetta pulled it away, and left her swinging. The ladder was too much for Rosetta, and she toppled backward against the table and upset the lamp, setting fire to the place quickly. The agile Lucia scrambled up to the shop, and as she lay crouching against the wall, she saw the fight. In a mad rush at the fast tiring boy, Luigi stumbled, and fell into the open trap, from which smoke was now issuing thickly. Pietro, insane with rage, the memory of the years of abuse welling in his fierce little heart, crouched at the opening, knife in hand. In the smoke of the cellar, Rosetta struggled to put back the ladder. She finally adjusted it, and Luigi, struggling to his knees, motioned her to ascend. Pietro helped her out and she fell unconscious on the floor of the shop. But when Luigi's fingers clutched the ledge, Pietro slashed at them — and they relaxed and were withdrawn; and when Luigi again attempted to climb up, Pietro shoved the ladder away from the opening and leaped down after it!

Luigi lay upon his face in the thick smoke of the cellar, and Pietro lay upon him, his boyish fingers sunk into his stepfather's throat. Of course, Graham and the policemen and many others had come in by this time, but the place was a mass of flame and smoke, and they barely got Lucia and old Rosetta out in safety. And in the smoke of the cellar, Pietro had his way with Luigi.

At the trial of Dimitri, Lucia proved the accuracy of her hearing. She picked out Dimitri's step among many. Dimitri didn't want to subject himself to the test; but his counsel, not believing in such things, and seeing that the effect would be very bad on the jury if he didn't, urged him to submit to the test. And he was sorry afterwards.

Graham had lingered after the trial to receive the congratulations of everybody. Lucia came into the library and Mrs. Arbuthnot was there. She had just been holding a letter up to the light and trying to see what it said. She handed the letter to Lucia and helped her read it. The letter was from " Max Marks, Incorporated," or somebody, offering Lucia $500 a week for ten weeks " because of her wonderful ability on the violin and on account of her place in the public eye." Lucia shrank from it.

" Of course, you will accept," said Mrs. Arbuthnot, " for you must feel that you should leave here at the earliest possible moment." Lucia went upstairs slowly and began to pack. Then she realized that she had brought nothing with her, except her violin, and could take nothing away. Graham came into the library, and Mrs. Arbuthnot told him of the circumstances and showed him the letter, and told him, also, that Miss Stryver said that the girl had been there too long already.

" Damn Miss Stryver! " said Graham, and then he proceeded to lay down the law in no uncertain terms, and Mrs. Arbuthnot left hurriedly. Graham stood at the table holding the letter when Lucia came in to say "Goodbye." He looked at her a long time without speaking. She came to him and sank on her knees before him and kissed his hand in humble gratitude, dropping her violin and her small bundle. He lifted her as one would a doll and put her into a chair. He kicked the bundle away, took off her hat and gloves, and put the violin in its accustomed place. Then he pointed at the letter, and though he said nothing, his face spoke — "What are you going to do about that?"

She looked long into his eyes and she saw there something that she had never seen before. Slowly she rose, still looking at him to be sure she read aright, and taking the letter, tore it in two. And then with a little gasp, she came into his open arms, and buried her face upon his breast.

CIRCUS MARY

Produced by The Universal Film Company.

Featuring MARY FULLER.

Directed by Lucius Henderson.

The Circus had come to town! There was no doubt about it. On every fence and wall were the posters with the prancing horses, the golden chariots, the lovely ladies poised and posed upon the trapezes, their lack of clothes being another sure indication that Spring had indeed come. There were the pictures of funny clowns and elephants twenty feet tall and giraffes thirty; the giant, and the fat and the bearded ladies; the complacent young woman who sat perfectly calm in a cage of lions that would have frightened Daniel out of his wits — and all the rest of " The Most Colossal Aggregation of Transcontinental and Stupendous Wonders Ever Gathered Together Under One Tent! " Small boys — and big ones — left their tops and marbles and other games; children stopped their fathers to look and marvel; and fathers stopped children, too, if the truth must be known, for about the same purpose. We never quite outgrow the Circus.

And on this day, twenty years ago, Mary, her face like a flower, and her form but ill concealed by the gauze and the spangles, sat upon the handsomest horse in the outfit, with Marsac, the Clown, at her side, and smiled at the yokels, as the horse did " High School " down the street, to the blatant tarara of the sweating band. Mary was " The Queen of the Air " with the show, and funny little Marsac, the Clown, had made her the Queen of his Heart, and he had laid it at her feet, I can't tell you how many times, or in how many strange places. Amid the sawdust of the ring, and before the tiger's cage, and as she fondled old Hector, the elephant, while his sensitive trunk searched her handbag for sugar plums, and lots of other places. Mary never would quite consent; for Mary was eighteen and good to look upon, and had the way of women. But Marsac always felt that he would rather be refused by her than accepted by anyone else — which is the way all true lovers should feel.

And then came John Hammond, a rising young attorney and politician, and completely upset everything, as far as Marsac was concerned, and Mary, too, for that matter. He met Mary —

was introduced by "The Old Man" — and he went to work very fast. There were a few dinners, a few moonlight walks; and then a carriage with horses which met Mary at the edge of the circus lot, late one night. And the next morning, Philadelphia papers told how John Hammond, about whom there had been some talk for the congressional nomination (the Boss had promised it to him), had married Miss Mary Elton, known as "The Queen of the Air," with Robbins's circus! And Marsac could only grit his teeth in his grief, and go on clowning, just the same.

After the honeymoon, Hammond took her to his fine home, and started to introduce her into society. After a number of distinct snubs, mostly from people who weren't fit to tie Mary's shoes, he gave it up. The Boss had to refuse him the congressional nomination on account of what he called "his escapade," and other cheerful things happened.

And poor Mary found out all about it. She felt that she was a millstone about her husband's neck; and after a night of tears, she stole quietly down the big stairs and out into the street — and back to the circus! Hammond was too proud to go after her, although he really loved her; but instead, he devoted himself to his profession, with excellent results.

They welcomed Mary back to the circus with open arms; the " Old Man " was jubilant; the Clown was exultantly happy, the freaks lost their grouches, and the animals got their sugar again. Months after her return, her baby was born, and for its little life, Mary gave her own. Poor Marsac stood at the bedside in the tent, the tears making furrows down his make-up; but the audience was calling for him, and he had to go on, dancing and grinning and tumbling about, just as though the wound in his heart wasn't bleeding a stream that would never be stopped. And after the last bow and grimace, he staggered back to her bed. Mary roused herself enough to take the Clown's hand and put it on the baby, and to whisper to him with her last breath, " I want you to promise me that you will always look out for my baby." And Marsac promised, and took the baby in his arms. And when they had covered Mary's face, the women of the circus came to Marsac, who stood with staring eyes, and tried to take the baby from him, but he would not let it go.

And all through the years, he never did let the baby go. He taught her little feet the road — always the right one — and she was his constant companion and playfellow. When she was four, he used to hold her on the steady old ring-horse, and on the little low wire that he rigged up; together they sat and fed and teased the big elephant with pop-corn and sugar. And always on Sundays, dressed in their best, he took her to church — money couldn't have bribed him to forego that duty, rain or shine. And at eighteen, Mary was the flower and pride of the circus — they called her "The Clown's Baby." Like her mother, whom she resembled strikingly, she was an adept on the high wire. She led the usual circus life, but always guarded by Marsac.

"The Old Man" was having a lot of trouble with the grafters who followed the show. One of them made love to Mary, and got so bold one day, that he tried to take her hand which lay in her lap under an apron. He didn't know that a pet snake's head lay in her lap also, until he took hold of it; and that ended Mr. Pedro's wooing for that day, at least. The Old Man broke up their shell game one time, when there was a particularly rich crop of " suckers " in sight, and a fight followed, during which one of the tent-men was shot. The police came and the District Attorney, young Mr. Graham. Two of the grafters had been captured.

When Graham questioned the circus people, Mary asserted positively that neither of the captured ones did the shooting. " Pedro shot the tent-man. I saw him." This made Mary a material witness, and it was arranged that she go to the District Attorney's office to make her statement in proper form.

They started with the police, but Graham's car developed engine trouble, and was delayed; and in a lonely stretch of road, Graham and Mary came across the fleeing remnant of Pedro's gang. And when it was all over, Mary and Graham lay bound on the upper floor of a big deserted factory, while Pedro and the gang debated on the lower floor what was to be done with them. Pedro's brother was one of the captured ones, and Pedro wanted to get him off. Mary managed to gnaw through the rope that bound Graham's hands, and then they were liberated enough to reconnoiter their position for possible chances of escape.

Near to the one window, high above the ground, ran some wires. Mary at once suggested that it would be easy for her, once she were on the wire, to walk to the pole and climb down. Graham wouldn't hear of it, at first; but Mary finally had her way; and after a good deal of difficulty, she swung from the window sill to the wire and walked away, while Graham watched her from the window. She got the police, and they rescued Graham, just in time, for he was having a desperate fight with the gang, but Pedro escaped, as desperate villains usually do.

Governor Hammond, formerly John Hammond, who ran away with "The Queen of the Air," twenty years before, passed a flaring circus bill on his way to the capitol. It was the same old circus, and there was another "Queen of the Air" confronting him; and memories crowded thick and fast upon him, and a mist came into his eyes as the one romance of his life came in vision before him. But he brushed it away with a sigh, and stopped in to congratulate young Graham, who was a particular friend and protégé of his, upon his narrow escape from a gang of desperate kidnappers.

"Governor," said Graham, "that girl saved my life. I want you to come to the circus this evening and see her perform." The Governor wouldn't hear of it at first; but after a good deal of persuasion, he finally agreed.

And so, that night, when Mary came tripping into the sawdust ring, bowing and smiling, the Governor, in his box, snatched the opera glasses from Graham's hand. Through them he saw his wife again, as he had first seen her, twenty years ago, and he gasped and swayed in his seat. There could be but one explanation — his wife must have had a daughter — this was no chance resemblance! He watched Mary climb the ladder to the little platform from which she stepped on the wire; but neither his eye nor any other saw Pedro, lurking back of the box, his knife in his hand and murder in his face. Mary did her evolutions on the wire, but in the midst of them, she saw, in the box, behind Graham and the Governor, Pedro's evil face, and his knife lifted to strike Graham in the back. She pointed and screamed; and Graham turned just in time to avoid the thrust. But Mary tottered on the wire, lost her balance, and fell.

Next to the Clown, Graham and the Governor were the first at her side. The Clown knew the Governor, and the Governor knew the Clown. This swept away the last doubt in his mind. "This is my daughter," the governor shouted. "Quick! Take her to my home!"

During the long days of convalescence, Mary had many a talk with her father, and with the "Old Man" and the Clown — to say nothing of Graham. Whenever they could, the "Old Man" and the Clown appeared at the door of the executive mansion, their rival bouquets in their hands, a little "bluffed" by the gorgeous butler who opened the door, but sure of a kindly welcome from Mary and the Governor. They were all there one morning, when Graham came in and, nodding to the others, went straight to Mary and began an animated conversation. Gradually the Governor, the " Old Man," and the Clown realized that they were distinctly out of it. The Governor winked at the Clown and the " Old Man," and jerked his head in the direction of the other room. They slipped out, entirely unobserved by Mary and Graham. Beside the big carven sideboard, the Governor, the " Old Man," and the Clown lifted up tall glasses of something cold and wet, and winked at each other. And when Mary and Graham discovered that they were alone, well, they took advantage of that fact, just as many a young couple has before, and undoubtedly will again.

THE LAST LEAF

In production by Edison Company.

In the long summer afternoons, and in the cool twilight, old Grandpa Holden used to sit upon the bench beside the door of his vine-clad cottage, his old dog at his feet, and look out over the broad expanse of ocean before him, and dream of the days when he was a stalwart fisherman among his fellows. His fellows! All gone now — Silas and Martin and Reuben and the rest — he was the last of them all — and yet it seemed but yesterday! Eighty years didn't seem long — when he looked back.

Mary, his little motherless granddaughter, who lived with him in the cottage, would come and light his pipe for him; and they would sit, her arm about him, and watch for the coming of Jacques — big, strong, handsome Jacques, who loved Mary and whom Mary loved. Indeed, there was no secret about it, and they were waiting only until Jacques could save enough to buy his fishing smack, and he had almost enough now. Jacques would come along the beach and stop at the cottage and leave the choicest of his catch for them. Grandpa would insist on taking the fish on the flimsy excuse that he alone could clean them properly, and bustle into the cottage, winking at Jacques as he went. Grandpa was not so old that he had forgotten that lovers like to be alone.

And moonlight nights, when Mary and Jacques strolled along the beach, he would come to the door and follow them with his eyes for a moment, as though to assure himself that no one had carried them off; then he would chuckle, rub his hands in satisfaction, look at the sky, and shuffle off to bed.

Sometimes he and Mary went down to the landing when the boats sailed in the morning; and often they were there, with the other folks of the village, when the boats returned. One morning, Grandpa came down to the landing and told the fishers that they better wait a while before setting out; for his discerning old eyes had seen something in the sky that he didn't like. But Jacques and the rest of the hardy young fellows laughed goodnaturedly at his fears, and sailed away, leaving Grandpa shaking his wise, gray head and tapping angrily with his cane. . . .

The fog came down upon the sea and the shore like a veil, and great waves beat against the rocky coast and the landing. Men looked into each other's faces, and could only walk the shore and blow the fog-horn, to which there was no answer. And the women — the wives and the sweethearts — could only sit and wait, and some wept, for that was their portion.

The boats never came back. And many days, Mary walked the beach, peering across the waters for a sight of her Jacques, who lay upon a floating spar, a hundred miles from any shore. Long after they knew hope had fled, Grandpa and the other old men of the village used to sail away in a " rescue " ship, anchor in some hidden cove, and smoke their pipes in gloomy silence, until it was time to return to the anxious women, for whose sake they sought what they knew they could never find!

And then, one night, as they sat before the drift-wood fire in the cottage, Grandpa told Mary that Jacques and his ship were only memories. She rose and stood a moment, wild-eyed, and then sank in a heap at his feet.

" Oh, Daddy," she sobbed, " Jacques must come! " The old man tenderly lifted her face in his hands and looked deep into her eyes — and she hid her face upon his breast.

Mary slowly disengaged herself from the old man's arms, and with bowed head went down to the beach and looked across the waters along the pathway of the moon. Surely that was Jacques who beckoned and opened his arms to her! " Yes, yes, Jacques, I am coming to you! "

She found the little boat and pushed out and threw away the oars. Jacques would guide her! Down and down the pathway of the moon she drifted — further and further from the shore — nearer and nearer to Jacques! And then, there was only the pathway of the moon across the illimitable sea. . . .

Many, many days, Grandpa used to hobble down to the shore with his old dog, and look across the waters. Then he would slowly turn away and retrace his steps — very feeble and faltering they were now, and the old dog followed on behind.

THE HEIR OF THE AGES

A Prologue and a Story
In Five Parts

Written for Mr. House Peters
by
William Addison Lathrop

———

Following is a complete scenario, "The Heir
of the Ages," in which is shown the synopsis,
scene-plot, cast, and the continuity. The continuity is the actual development of the story
into scenes from which the director builds the
picture.

The theory of Transmission of Souls is too
well known to need any comment, and whether
it be true or not has nothing to do with this
story. We do know, however, that certain traits,
both physical and mental, are transmitted or
handed down from generation to generation,
and there often appear what are called atavisms,
or reversions to a type far remote in the
line of ancestry. The dog and the cat turn
around several times before lying down, simply

Mr. House Peters

because for thousands of years their ancestors, the wolf and the tiger, turned around in exactly the same manner, to press down the grass and rushes of the jungle into a comfortable bed. A lion, born in captivity, will become infuriated at the squeak of a monkey, though he has never seen a monkey; because there is a cell somewhere in his brain which tells him that monkeys annoyed his ancestors. We all have flashes, usually in dreams, fragmentary and vague, of a dim and distant past, inexplicable on any other ground than as a heritage of the years. Type recurrences are frequent and unmistakable. Who shall say that they are *not* identities? It is upon these premises that this story is based.

Way back in the ages, when Time was young, and the giant forces of nature were still at work wrinkling up the surface of the cooling globe into mountains, and gouging out holes for the seas, there lived The Man. He had already learned to walk erect, and seldom now took to the trees; he had learned to make a fire, and he knew how to use a few tools such as a bow and arrow and a paddle and a stone hatchet. He lived in a cave far up a cliff. He was beset with dangers of the most appalling kind at all times, and eternal vigilance was the price of his life. He was tall and strong; long of limb and

lithe; and upon his body he wore the skins of
the animals he had slain, and upon his feet he
had already begun to wear sandals with a thong
that laced them to his ankles and calves — he
didn't use his feet like an extra pair of hands
any longer, and he could protect them.

This particular Man had a brother who lived
in the cave with him — a slender stripling of
some seventeen or eighteen years. The Brother
was a weakling — as weaklings went in those
days. The Man loved him and protected him,
and did things for him so often that The Brother
got to expect it as a right, and probably that was
one reason why he was weak. Human emotions
were few in those days; Hate and Fear and Lust
and Greed were about the gamut; and that made it
all the more remarkable that The Man should
sacrifice himself for anybody. But all things
have a beginning, and maybe this was the beginning of Self-Sacrifice. The Man went out into
the countless dangers of the forest and the
mountain, killed and brought home the game;
then he cooked it, after he had made a fire —
which was a tough job, rubbing two sticks
together — and then The Brother ate his own
share and usually part of The Man's. The Man
instructed his Brother in the use of the bow and
the club and the hatchet, but he never seemed to
get to the point where he could care for himself.

One day as he came through the tall grasses of the jungle, The Man saw The Girl. He watched her for some time from behind a tree, while she platted the grasses into some new style of skirt and looked at the effect in the clear waters of the stream.

The Man decided that he wanted her, and therefore he took her. She bit his arm with her sharp, white teeth when he grabbed her; but he didn't mind that (tetanus hadn't been invented then), and he bore her away, kicking and squalling; that was the way courting was done in those days. I am afraid that she didn't kick or squall quite as lustily as she could, either. But it was enough to bring to her side two of her tribe who gave The Man battle, while she looked on, with plenty of chance to run away if she had really cared to do so.

The battle was a very unequal one; The Man laid out his adversaries so that subsequent proceedings were of no interest to them; though one of them might have got away, had not the lady tripped him. Anyway, The Man bore off The Girl in triumph to the cave.

But no sooner did Brother see her, than he wanted her. For a moment, it was a toss-up whether The Man would wring Brother's neck, or beat his head in with a twenty-five pound club. But The Girl settled it by showing a decided preference for Brother. And so, although it was a pretty tough struggle, he let Brother have her.

But "When Poverty comes in at the door, Love flies out of the window." That was just as true then as it is now, only they didn't put it that way. They found that they still had to depend upon The Man, not only for food, but for protection; and as a brave man is always a fine sight, The Girl began to look with more and more contempt upon her husband, and with more and more favor upon The Man — but The Man would have none of her.

It was, as I have said, a time when cataclysms of Nature were frequent, and one day The Man stood upon a high crag, and saw the elements conspire for the destruction of the world. Before they knew it, the Deluge was upon them. He saw his Brother and The Girl run in terror along the rocky shore; and out of force of habit, perhaps, he went to their aid. He hid them beneath the shelving rock, The Brother crouching in terror, while The Girl clung to The Man's tunic, and the lightnings played about them; and The Man was not afraid.

They came to the last refuge, a rock that rose from the sea and across which the surf dashed in pitiless fury. There upon the rock, The Man placed them. Even muscles like his can be exhausted, and he felt his hold slipping. The

Brother only crouched and shivered in terror. But The Girl, perhaps the first of her race to feel the touch of Human Sympathy for other than her own flesh and blood, reached down to help The Man as he buffeted the storm. And when his hold loosened and he slipped down into the black waters, she leaped from the rock with opened, eager arms that clasped about his neck, and eyes that looked into his — perhaps for Eternity.

THE STORY

Time unrolled the scroll of the year until a million, or more, if you will, had passed. The world was old and gray now, and the same forces of Nature, with wonderful alchemy, had wrinkled up the Sierras and the Rockies, and had hid gold in their bosoms for men to find. Some discouraged prospectors had struck a rich vein when they were about ready to quit, but had tried " just once more," and a town had sprung up like a mushroom in the night. They called the town Last Chance.

Hugh Payne, superintendent of The Golconda, sat in his bungalow, which was only a little better than a shack, at least outside, buried deep in a book. The room was filled with books and rugs and heads and skins, appointments of luxury in that place. From the windows he could see the town below, with the usual streets of saloons and dance halls; with its " Forty-Second St. and Broadway," " St. Regis," " Delmonico's," " Eat Here and Die Outside," and kindred expressions of humor.

The principal place where a variety of evil things could be indulged in was called " The Square Deal." It was run by one Kearney, a semi-handsome and totally depraved scoundrel, who made it his business to pander to as many vices as it is possible to crowd under one roof.

Among the bedraggled and bedecked harlots that frequented the place was one who bore the sobriquet of " The Duchess." She stood out among the others like a diamond in a coal heap. Her perfect, beautiful face, with its ingenuous, baby stare, concealed a disposition and morals that would have shocked Messalina. Kearney exercised a sort of proprietorship over her, though his tenure was never very secure, and in one way or another, she was the real boss of the place. She would order a drink, and if it didn't quite suit her fancy, she would dash glass and all into the waiter's face, and smile seraphically as she watched someone wipe the blood from the wounded man — and no one said her nay.

The dive and the town were about as sordid and as interesting as such dives and towns usually are. But there were certain people about to come to town who made it interesting enough. Along the steep mountain trail came Penelope Agatha Spottiswoode Hope — she was about five feet three, with all that name! When people had known her five minutes, they called her " Missy " — everybody did.

With Missy were a pack mule and Missy's father, Beverly Hope, a sad and negative little man, the gentlest, most submissive thing in the world — to Missy — but of a sort that is hardly worth putting into a census. He had always been a prospector, and always would be; his one aim in life being to acquire enough to live miserably and to keep " pickled," as Missy put it. Missy was exactly the opposite — bright, pretty, energetic, ragged, and seventeen.

The Hopes took domicile in an old, abandoned cabin in the hills; Beverly patching it up a little outside, and Missy making the inside almost inviting with her feminine touch. They didn't really expect callers, though they had created a mild sensation as they went through the town, and the Duchess and some of the other girls had quite a laugh, much to Missy's indignation.

But they had a caller, very soon, and a most important one. Hugh Payne, having settled a quarrel at the mine between two men who had drawn knives, but who didn't really want to fight — Hugh told them that if they ever started anything again he would make them fight — rode idly down the trail. Near the spring, he saw Missy, who was arranging her hair and her dress after the manner of a fashion sheet of a magazine she had found in the abandoned shack, and admiring her reflection in the water. Hugh didn't know of Missy's existence until that minute; but after he had watched her for a time, he rode up and startled her not a little. But Missy was used to men, and in a few moments Hugh had dismounted and they were sitting on the ground near the spring, talking with great interest. It was some time before Hope came back to the cabin and called Missy. She started up and was going home without the water for which she had come. Hugh called attention to the empty bucket, and they had a great laugh. Hugh filled it, and they started away again, and this time Missy called Hugh's attention to the fact that he had forgotten the horse; he went back and got it; and leading the horse and carrying the pail, Hugh came back to the cabin with the girl.

Old Man Hope invited him in hospitably, and Hugh accepted. He noticed a small shelf of books, four in all, and asked Missy if she were

fond of them. " O, yes, indeed," said Missy.
Hugh asked her which of the four she preferred,
and after some hesitation, she indicated her
favorite. Hugh took out the volume and saw
that the title was " Geodetic Survey of Arizona."
He was puzzled, but Missy changed the subject
cleverly; and soon they were seated with Old Man
Hope by the fire, who talked to Hugh glibly,
though it must be confessed that Hugh was so
absorbed in looking at Missy that once or twice
some slight confusion resulted from his replies
to the questions of Mr. Hope.

Back East, Larry Payne, Hugh's younger
brother, was making ducks and drakes of the
last of his fortune. He came out, in pajamas
and dressing-gown, into his sitting room, this
morning, and it had evidently been a rough night.
He sat in his chair, after Higgins, the valet, had
mixed a couple of cocktails, and thought it over.
It was a jumble of poker, wine, ladies, and automobiles. Higgins interrupted the dream by saying, apologetically, " Beg pawdon, Mr. Payne,
Sir, but several of these people are getting quite
importunate, Sir." (Larry had just thrown a
package of mail, all bills, into the waste basket.)
" In fact, I might say, beggin' your pawdon,
Sir, violent."

Then the telephone rang, before Larry could
reply, and Higgins, in response to a frantic wave

of Larry's hand, said that Larry was not in. The person at the other end must have said something altogether unpleasant, for Higgins hung up the receiver with a shocked air. "Never mind," said Larry, "I'll write to Brother Hugh if I get time today and he'll come across with enough to tide me over until I can get that mortgage through." Higgins had to be satisfied with that, and Larry lapsed again into revery.

The letter to "Brother Hugh" came in due time, and when Hugh got it he was in ill humor. He read it as he was passing the Square Deal and Kearney hailed him: "What's the trouble, Payne? Bad news? Come in and have a drink." Hugh looked slowly up from the letter; then, walking close to the man, he said, "*Mr.* Payne for yours, Kearney. Yes, very bad news. I've got a younger brother who is being speeded on his way to hell by just such scoundrels as you. Come along, I'll go you on that drink."

Hugh had never been in the Square Deal before, and his entrance caused no little sensation. "The Duchess" spotted him from afar and marked him for her own. He stood at the bar — he wasn't a drinker, but you never can tell what a Cave Man will do — and drank half a dozen drinks, for which he paid, denying Kearney that privilege.

Then "The Duchess" joined them; she put

her baby face up to Hugh's and said impudently,
" So, you've dropped in to see us at last, Mr.
Goliath. We thought you were a woman-hating
prohibitionist." Hugh looked at her gravely and
steadily, and she was uncomfortable under his
gaze. Then he deliberately drained his glass,
looking over her head.

" Kearney," he said, " if this lady is a friend
of yours, you better advise her to withdraw, as
I'm about to start something."

Over at adjoining tables were the two miners
who had evinced a desire to fight a few days
before. They were belligerent again, but it
seemed unlikely that they would come to blows.
Hugh walked over to them — they saw him too
late — though they tried to get away. Hugh
grabbed them, hurled them to the floor, flung
the tables and chairs away until he had cleared
a space, making havoc with the furniture, and
then — well, he made them fight. As either
showed signs of quitting, one look at Hugh made
him go at the other man, instead of taking a
chance with " The Cave Man." Two or three
who attempted to interfere were glad enough to
get away alive — Kearney knew too much to try
it — and the most interested spectator was " The
Duchess "! From that moment, she belonged to
Hugh, body and soul — and all the more because
he ignored her. And when Nero was through

with his Roman Holiday, he walked out of the place. And he had left an impression. Yet he could not have told you why he did it!

Midnight found him drawing a cheque for five hundred dollars to Brother's order. He wrote several letters to accompany it, but he tore them up in turn, and sent the cheque alone in the envelope.

Meanwhile, Hugh had brought Missy an armful of books, carefully selected. One morning, she decided to return them. She came to Hugh's bungalow, gay in new shoes, stockings, and gown, bright and early in the morning. She knocked and got no response. She went around and climbed into the window. She liked the place, first rate, and examined most of the things. Then she started toward the inner door; Hugh, who had been awakened, called out, asking who was there.

" It's me," said Missy, regardless of Lindley Murray, " can I come in? " Hugh bounced out of bed and braced himself against the door in a panic. He shouted directions to her through the closed door, and Missy sat down to wait. He came out, and she told him that she had brought back the books and that they were " lovely."

" Which did you like best? " asked Hugh. Missy selected one from the lot and opened it embarrassedly. Hugh asked her to read from it to him; she looked at him in mute helplessness — the book was upside down in her hands! Missy bowed her poor little head upon the table, and Hugh felt like the big brute he was.

And so it was agreed that Hugh should undertake her education; and spurred on by the inspiration of love, she was an apt pupil. Old Man Hope was pressed into service by the insistent Missy, though he would much rather have been at the Square Deal. Occasionally he did manage to get away. He came stumbling home one time when Hugh was before the cabin with Missy at the daily lesson. He was extravagantly polite to Hugh and to Missy, but he stubbed his toe getting into the cabin.

" No," said Missy, in answer to Hugh's inquiring look, " I don't reckon I need any help. He's always gentle and minds me like a child, but I can't watch him all the time. When he gets good and pickled, he quits for a while. He'll be good now for a spell, for he's sure plastered."

Often, Hope tried to get out, after Missy had gone up the ladder to her bed in the loft. Usually, when he decided that the coast was clear and was tip-toeing across the floor, with his hat on and his boots in his hand, on his way to the Square Deal, Missy, in her night dress, would appear at the top of the ladder; and the Old Man would cough apologetically, march straight back, and begin to undress in earnest. And all the while, the bond between Hugh and Missy grew stronger and stronger — there was something of the Cave People in each.

And just at this time, Last Chance had an important addition to its population — Larry! The Sheriff was getting too close for comfort in New York, and he decided that the West offered opportunities to a youth of his talents and proclivities.

It did. He blew in on Hugh one evening at the bungalow, and Hugh was genuinely glad to see him; especially after Larry said that he had come West to make a man of himself and wanted a job. Larry had stopped at the Square Deal on his way up to Hugh's cottage, and had made himself popular at once — and with "The Duchess," too. Kearney didn't like it much, but he realized that it was only the usual process of skinning a "sucker," and let it go at that. But that wasn't right — "The Duchess" was shooting high, and she considered the Paynes about the right sort for her to tie to.

Then came a telegram calling Hugh to the main offices of the mine in San Francisco — Larry was in possession. And he made a lot of use of it. The next morning, as he sat at breakfast, in walked Missy with some books. They looked at each other in astonishment.

Larry recovered first. " All the comforts of a home! " quoth he. " Hugh certainly has a nice place! " He swept the little mountain girl off her feet with his voluble attentions; and at length, after she had declined an invitation to sit down and visit, or to have a little breakfast, or a drink, or something, he decided that she must have some more books, and he elected himself to select them and to carry them to her home for her. And inside of half an hour, he was sitting perfectly at ease before Missy's cabin, in Hugh's old place, telling the bewildered but pleased Missy all about New York and the tall buildings, and what a devil of a fellow he was.

Evenings — the early part, that is — would find him at the Hope cabin with a line of entertaining conversation, which Old Man Hope enjoyed. When he left, Missy went to the dooryard with him, and he pointed out the big bright stars and told her that her eyes made them look foolish. And after a month — in which the accomplished city man wooed the simple little girl of the mountains with all the arts at his command — he hadn't made a dent in the armor of her love for Hugh, though the ass thought she was his for the asking!

The latter part of the evenings he spent at the Square Deal. He played a little roulette, with " The Duchess " standing back of his chair; and put down a bet for her now and then, which always won, and she rewarded him with a kiss — much to Kearney's disgust. And he made himself, withal, "a good fellow."

Finally, when he thought the time was ripe, he asked Missy to marry him. She ran away from him laughing; but Larry put it down to bashful maidenhood — she didn't say "No," anyway, and he was satisfied that she was his.

That night, when Hugh got home — he had been wrestling with gray-haired directors in Frisco until he had brought them to his way of thinking — and was just sitting down to a bountiful dinner that the Chink had prepared, Larry cut in — "Old Man, I have some news for you, that I'm sure you'll be glad to hear. You often said that the best thing I could do would be to marry: that it would steady me. I'm going to take your advice. I'm going to marry Missy Hope. I know she is rather below us, but she's the goods."

Hugh was toying with a fork; he stopped and looked at Larry. Right there, Larry never knew how close he came to being strangled; but The Man smothered the volcano within him.

At length he said, "Have you asked her?"

Larry laughed. "Yes," he said, "and she didn't say 'No.'" Slowly the old instinct of self-sacrifice and love for his brother gained the mastery; and through the Strong Man's brain there flitted the dim and shadowy echo of a memory — it was something about a cave wherein a young man and a young woman looked into each other's faces, and a big strong man turned slowly away and went out into the night.

The volatile Larry, wrapped in himself, did not notice the volcano within his brother; and with a cheery " So long! I'm off to see her now," he left, after selecting a few books to take with him.

The dinner was untouched; the Chinaman pussy-footed in, but he took one good look at Hugh, and pussy-footed right out. And when Hugh came back to himself, the heavy silver fork was twisted and knotted in his powerful hands.

And that night, as Hugh strode aimlessly through the woods, crashing into things, he got what seemed to him confirmation. He saw Missy and Larry before the Hope cabin, the light from the open door behind them. They were so far away that he could not hear what was said. Larry was talking earnestly to Missy and was holding her hands, while she looked up into his face. Hugh turned away, sick at heart.

And yet, if he could only have heard, Missy was telling Larry that " she didn't care for him that way, and that he mustn't ask her again! "

Larry went straight from Missy to the Square Deal!

Hugh, in the shadows, saw him go down the trail to the town, and followed him without knowing why. Missy went back into the cabin and Old Man Hope was not there! He had taken the opportunity to slip out, and Missy started out determinedly to collect him and " cash him in." And so the three came to the Square Deal. Larry came first; there were few there — Kearney being among those absent. Larry inquired for " The Duchess;" she was upstairs in her room, the girls told him. Larry took a chance and went up, though he knew that Kearney would murder him if he were caught. He found " The Duchess " preening herself for the evening's conquests, and she welcomed and admired his temerity. Hugh had seen Larry go into the saloon, and he followed, wondering. A man at the bar told him that Larry had gone upstairs to see " The Duchess," and that there would very probably be quite a little excitement if Kearney came in. Hugh left his drink untasted, and strode up the stairs.

He had hardly disappeared, when Missy came in timidly, looking for her father. The girls gathered round her; one of them said, " Why don't you go upstairs and see your friend, Mr. Payne? He is calling on ' The Duchess '! "

Missy said it was a lie; but the girls told her that she better go up to see. There was a little of The Cave Woman in Missy, and she went. Hugh had opened the door of " The Duchess' " room, and there were she and Larry in animated conversation. Hugh said nothing, only looked. Larry stammered some kind of excuse, and Hugh came into the room and Larry and " The Duchess " turned to him, for his face was ominous.

Then at the door, appeared Missy. She saw them all, but none save Hugh saw her. The old instinct again — he must " cover " Larry! Hugh put his arm about " The Duchess " and said to Larry, " No, Larry, I won't go home with you. You have no right to interfere with me. This is my girl and I'm going to stay here! "

Missy stepped into the room and they all saw her now. " The Duchess " nestled comfortably against Hugh's broad breast. There was horror in Missy's eyes as she heard and saw. She looked at Hugh for a moment, and then, covering her face with her hands, she fled from the room. At a sign from Hugh, Larry slunk after her.

Once they were gone, Hugh flung " The Duchess " from him. It is probable that in her infatuation for him, she really thought Hugh meant what he said! But as she lay on the floor, she looked at him and read the truth in his face — and she admired him all the more! Kearney burst into the room with drawn revolver, and there was little doubt that he intended to use it. Hugh looked calmly at him, and he raged. There is always something very disconcerting to a coward in a brave man's steady, unfearing look. This was no exception, and Kearney felt his nerve slipping; he was bluffed, and he knew it.

" Kearney," said Hugh calmly, " if you ever shot me with that thing and I found it out, I might do you some harm. Better put it up before I take it away from you. I'm leaving now. You didn't think " (indicating " The Duchess ") " that I wanted that — carrion, did you? " And he strode out of the room, turning his back upon the raging Kearney.

Kearney looked at " The Duchess," and there was no mistaking the contempt in her face — or in her words, either — she said something about " class " telling. With an oath, the spell having been broken, Kearney rushed after Hugh. He had gone part way across the dance floor which was now crowded, many having heard of the mix-up and come in through curiosity. Missy was looking for her father, of whom she had caught a glimpse, and Larry was trying to make up his mind to tell Missy the truth about the whole affair.

Kearney ran part way down the stairs and fired at Hugh. Hugh turned, the Cave Man in him aroused, and dashed back toward the stairs up which Kearney retreated before him, firing again. Hugh kept right on and Kearney ran along the hall and into " The Duchess's " room, Hugh after him. There was pandemonium in the big hall. Larry had managed to make Missy understand that it was he who was the renegade, and that Hugh had come there to save him. Score one decent thing for Larry. Missy went frantic.

" He came here to save you — why don't you try to save him — or let me? " and she tried to get to Hugh up the stairs, but Larry held her, afraid to go himself! In " The Duchess's " room Kearney dodged around, and " The Duchess " ran toward Hugh to protect him. Kearney shot, and " The Duchess " fell. Hugh turned to look at her and Kearney took careful aim; but " The Duchess," half rising, grasped a lamp from the table and threw it at Kearney, and the room was dark, save the dim light from the hall. There was the flash of the pistol, but in the dim shadows, silhouetted in the gloom, " The Duchess " saw, with closing eyes, Hugh's hands close on Kearney's throat, and with her dying ears she heard bones crack under the grip of the giant.

The flames started, but Hugh did not let go until he knew that Kearney would never trouble anybody again; and by that time the room was full of smoke. He bent over "The Duchess," and he knew that she was dead. He groped his way to the hall, carrying the dead woman. In the panic in the dance hall, Larry had been knocked down, and Missy was hemmed in by an overturned table, while men scrambled over them.

Hugh fought his way out to the street, and Old Man Hope came up with shrieking treble, and told him that Larry and Missy were still in the furnace. Hugh fought his way back, and groped in the smoke and flame and falling timbers till he found them. A beam had fallen across Larry, but Hugh brushed it aside, and taking Larry and the unconscious Missy in his arms, he staggered toward the door. Across his blinded vision, there came the dim and shadowy picture of a rock in the Deluge, and upon it a Man placed a Youth and a Girl. Only the thousandth part of a second did he see it, and it was vague and dim.

He got to the open air, how, he never knew, and fiercely rejecting all offers of assistance, he gently laid his burdens down. Larry lay, very white and still, but to Missy there came returning consciousness. Hugh looked upon the dead face of his Brother, and agony came into his eyes. Missy crawled to his feet; and on her knees, she took his hand in hers. Hugh looked into her face, and each knew that the other understood.

THE HEIR OF THE AGES

THE CHARACTERS

IN THE PROLOGUE

THE MAN
HIS BROTHER
THE GIRL
TWO SAVAGES AND A WOMAN

IN THE STORY

HUGH PAYNE...............An Atavism. Superintendent of the Golconda mine in Last Chance, California

PENELOPE AGATHA SPOTTISWOODE HOPE...... Known to everybody as "Missy." Seventeen, and daughter of a mining prospector.

LARRY PAYNE.............Hugh's brother. A type.

THE DUCHESS............."A lady with a character and gown decollete"

KEARNEY................. A semi-handsome and totally depraved scoundrel, proprietor of The Square Deal Saloon, Gambling Joint and Dance Hall. (And worse.)

OLD MAN HOPE...........Missy's father

SHORTY...................A hanger-on at The Square Deal

HIGGINS..................Larry's valet

SING LEE.................Hugh's cook

Foreman of the Mine, Miners, People at The Square Deal—men and girls—Board of Directors, Waiters, Bartender

SCENE-PLOT

Scenes in Prologue.

Interior of cave—15, 16, 17, 36, 38, 39, 40, 41, 42, 44.

All other scenes in Prologue are picturesque exteriors.

Scenes in Story.

Interior. Hugh's cabin—62, 63, 64, 121, 122, 123, 131, 133, 135, 137, 157, 159, 170, 171, 172, 173.

Interior. Hugh's bedroom—129, 132, 134, 136.

Exterior. Hugh's cabin—128, 130.

Exterior. Street in mining town—65, 82, 83, 84, 85, 86, 113, 114, 139, 140, 141, 142, 143, 144 145, 146, 147, 148, 183.

Exterior. Square Deal Saloon—66, 67, 68, 69, 70, 71, 72, 120, 138, 149, 155, 190, 201a, 204, 206, 207.

Interior. Square Deal Saloon—73, 74, 75, 76, 77, 115, 116, 117, 118, 119, 156, 167, 186, 189, 192, 193, 195, 198, 199, 201, 202, 203, 205.

Exterior. Mountain trails—78, 79, 80, 81, 97, 100, 127, 159, 181, 182, 184.

Exterior. Picturesque spots, the spring, etc.—98, 99, 101, 102, 103, 105, 169, 174.

Exterior. Hope's cabin and nearby trail—87, 96, 104, 106, 124, 150, 161, 165, 175, 177, 178, 179.

Interior. Hope's cabin—88, 89, 107, 108, 109, 110, 111, 112, 125, 151, 152, 153, 154, 164, 166, 176, 180.

Interior. The Duchess' room—185, 188, 194, 197, 198a.

Interior. Hall outside Duchess' room—187, 191, 196, 200.

Exterior. Railroad station—162, 163.

Exterior. Mining offices—90, 95.

Exterior. Near shaft—91, 92, 93, 94, 160.

Interior. Any large room—168.

Exterior. Street in suburbs of any city—112d.

Interior. Larry's rooms in New York—112a, 112c, 112e, 126.

Interior. Any handsomely furnished room for vision in Scene 112b.

CONTINUITY

Sub-Title. WHEN THE WORLD WAS YOUNG.

Scene 1. Vast and cragged rocks. Far view.

Scene 2. The jungle—wild and picturesque.

Scene 3. Any striking scenes of wild and picturesque nature—water-fall, distant smoking volcano, etc. (Probably many such scenes are in stock.) One or two scenes of the ocean; the surf beating, etc.

Scene 4. Huge serpent crawls among the rocks. Flash. Near view.

Scene 5. Repeat flash of 4, another location.

Scene 6. Lion prowls in jungle. Near view. (Any wild animal—in fact, if too difficult to obtain, the animal scenes may be omitted, though they would undoubtedly give color to the picture.)

Scene 7. At the drinking pool. Night. Picturesque pool in glade. Animals drink at pool. Far and near views.

Scene 8. Far view of high cliffs. Flash. Night.

Scene 9. Base of cliffs. Night. Wild animal prowls. Near view. Flash. Fade out.

Scene 10. Interior. Cave. Open diaphragm to near-view of The Man as he bends over the dried leaves, starting fire by friction; hold a few feet, then open to His Brother half reclining on floor of cave watching;

hold a few feet, then open to full view of interior of cave; both men clad in skins and sandals; bows and arrows, clubs, skins, etc. One duck by fire; as soon as fire is started, man prepares to cook the duck.

Scene 11. Flash of lion as he prowls at foot of cliff. Night. Same as 9.

Scene 12. Interior. Cave, same as 10. Night. Light from fire. Full view. Man hears animal; rises and goes to mouth of cave, followed by His Brother, who is plainly timid.

Scene 13. Near view of mouth of cave taken from without. Night. Main light from behind; partial light on the two faces. The Man stands, club in hand at mouth of cave, looking out into the night; behind him cowers His Brother, manifestly afraid, but with confidence in The Man.

Scene 14. Base of cliff, same as 9. Night. Flash. Lion turns away.

Scene 15. Interior. Cave, same as 10. Light from fire. Man and His Brother return to fire from mouth of cave; The Man cooks the duck.

Sub-Title. THE BEGINNING OF UNSELFISHNESS.

Scene 16. Interior. Cave, same as 10. Near view. Night. Light from fire. Man and His Brother eating duck; Brother has finished his share; looks enviously at the portion The Man still has; crawls nearer and asks for it. Man considers for some time, then hands it to Brother, who devours it greedily. Man looks at him, conflicting emotions in his face. Cut in a close-up of each. Then back to scene. The duck finished, Brother composes himself to sleep; Man sits, his back against wall of cave, looking at him.

Scene 17. Close-up. Cave, same as 10. The Man sits,

back against wall, as in 16, watching his brother. Fade out slowly.

Sub-Title. HIS BROTHER'S KEEPER.

Scene 18. Exterior. In the thick woods. The Man and His Brother come into picture and go through woods, The Man guiding and instructing His Brother, each has club and bow and arrows.

Scene 19. Exterior. Edge of swamp. Brother wants to explore swamp; Man prevents him, explaining dangers. (If thought effective, the particular dangers may be shown in visions as The Man talks.)

Scene 20. Exterior. In woods. Deer feed. Flash. Far view.

Scene 21. Exterior. Another part of woods. Flash. Figures near camera. The Man and His Brother steal upon the deer. The Man coaching Brother.

Scene 22. Exterior. Deer, as in 20. Flash. Near view.

Scene 23. Exterior. In woods. Near view. Flash. The Man points, and His Brother shoots.

Scene 24. Exterior. In woods, same as 20. Near view. Deer lies pierced by arrow; Brother and Man run into picture; Brother greatly pleased; Man shoulders deer and they go.

Sub-Title. "GIN A BODY MEET A BODY, COMIN' THROUGH THE RYE."

Scene 25. Exterior. In the jungle. Far view. Flash. The girl.

Scene 26. Exterior. Jungle. Near view. The Girl, idling, or adorning herself; she starts away.

Scene 27. Exterior. In the tall grass. The Girl comes through grass; sits and weaves grasses.

Scene 28. Exterior. In the woods. Flash. The Man strides through the woods; listens; changes his direction.

Scene 29. Exterior. Same as 27. Near view. The Girl gathers and weaves the grasses; starts and crouches at sound.

Scene 30. Exterior. At edge of grass. Near view. Flash. The Man looks intently; then starts into grass.

Scene 31. Exterior. Same as 27. Near view. The Girl crouches, startled, yet curious; The Man comes through the grass and stands over her, regarding her intently; cut in a close-up of each. Then back to scene. The Man approaches very slowly, his face smilingly interested and inquisitive; The Girl alert and ready to run, but also interestedly inquisitive; cut-in close-up flashes of the varying expression. Back to scene. As The Man gets too close for safety, The Girl starts to run, but is not quick enough, and he grabs her by the arm; she turns upon him and sinks her teeth in his arm. Cut in close-up of Girl biting his arm. Back to scene. The Man is not affected by the bite and pulls her face away from his arm and holds her off, regarding her as she struggles; after a moment, her struggles cease, she seeing that they are useless; she tries tears and The Man relents a little, loosening his hold; she tries to dart away, but again he is too quick, and catches her; shaking her in punishment; she seems subdued; after thinking the matter over for a time, he starts to drag her away; again she fights and screams, but The Man is not affected by this, and drags her out of picture, screaming, biting, and struggling.

Scene 32. Exterior. Base of a cliff. Figures near

camera. Two men about to climb cliff, when woman
rushes to them and jabbers and points; the men run
in the direction in which she points.

Scene 33. Exterior. Glade in woods. The Man comes
into picture, dragging Girl; finally picks her up and
carries her; she has ceased to struggle. Cut in close-up
of The Man with The Girl in his arms. Back to scene.
Part way through the glade, he stops to listen; drops
her on the ground, and faces about with club, belligerent. Cut in a near-view as he stands ready for the
attack, The Girl crouching at his feet, not availing
herself of the opportunity to get away which is offered.

Scene 34. Exterior. Near view. In forest. Flash. The
two men peer from behind tree, and prepare for the
attack; they start.

Scene 35. Exterior. In the glade, same as 33. The
Man and The Girl on, as in 33; the two men advance
and attack; the fight. (It is, perhaps, idle to supply
detail for a scene of this character, the locus and the
personnel of the actors are too variable factors, and
the detail must be supplied at the time of taking; suffice it, that The Man kills the two pursuers); The Girl
watches, a most interested spectator; possibly, to exem-
plify the early feminine disposition, *she might help
The Man a little;* and at the finish, goes with him will-
ingly enough, though she does not let him suspect it.
Cut in close-ups or near views of the main action and
of The Girl as she watches.

Scene 36. Interior. Cave, same as 10. Flash. The
Brother restless and nervous, goes to mouth of cave;
looks out; returns.

Scene 37. Base of cliff, same as 9. Exterior. The Man
and The Girl come into picture; she timid and making

half-hearted resistance; he starts to drag her up the cliff.

Scene 38. Interior. Cave, same as 10. Boy sits, expectant; The Man and The Girl enter, he dragging her in; she falls in a heap on the floor of cave; The Brother, on hands and knees, looks at her inquisitively.

Scene 39. Close-up of Brother as he looks at Girl. Flash.

Scene 40. Close-up of The Man as he looks at both. Flash.

Scene 41. Close-up of The Girl, as she peeks through her fingers at them.

Scene 42. Interior. Cave, same as 10. Near view. Man, Brother, and Girl on, as in 38; The Girl gradually assumes a sitting position and uncovering her eyes, looks at them; her gaze turns from The Man to the Brother, and as she looks at him, her face assumes a pleased expression, and she is plainly partial to the Brother. She allows him to touch her hand, and is not displeased with the caress; they each seem unconscious of The Man, who is regarding them gravely, his face darkening as the tête-á-tête progresses; once or twice, The Man starts as though to tear them both into pieces, but controls himself; once or twice, also, The Man starts to make advances toward The Girl, and she shrinks from him, plainly evincing her preference; at length, The Man slowly turns and goes, pausing at the mouth of the cave to look back at the girl clinging to the arm of The Brother who has assumed a new air — the air of a protector having found someone weaker than himself. Cut scene with close-ups of the main action.

Scene 43. Exterior. Base of cliff, same as 9. Night.

Near view. The Man comes into picture from above; stands with grave and saddened face. *Fade out.*

Leader. BUT VERY SOON, EVEN IN THE HONEYMOON, THEY FOUND THAT THEY MUST DEPEND UPON THE MAN.

Scene 44. Interior. Cave, same as 10. Full view. The Brother and The Girl in evident distress, she explaining pitifully that there is no food; he shows her his broken bow and explains that he cannot make a new one. The Man enters, carrying a deer which he drops at her feet; The Brother is delighted; shows The Man the broken bow, and The Man gives him his; The Girl looks a little pityingly at the Brother, and admiringly at The Man, who turns and goes, she following him with her eyes. Diaphragm out on her face.

Sub-Title. PRIMITIVE CHIVALRY.

Scene 45. Exterior. In the forest. The Brother and The Girl on; he in terror and inclined to hide behind her. A savage man approaches, evidently with evil intent; The Man rushes upon the scene, and the savage skulks away. The Brother greatly relieved; Girl looks with contempt upon The Brother and admiringly at The Man, who turns away; as The Brother leads away The Girl, she looks back at The Man. Diaphragm out on her face.

Leader. THE WORLD WAS STILL IN THE MAKING, AND NATURE'S MIGHTY FORCES WERE AT WORK.

Sub-Title. THE DELUGE.

Scene 46. Flash of the rocks lashed by the rising water.

Scene 47. Exterior. High crag. Figure near camera. The Man sees the storm unafraid.

Scene 48. Exterior. Flash of The Brother and The Girl running along rocky shore, in terror.

Scene 49. Exterior. High crag, same as 47. The Man sees Brother and Girl and starts to help them.

Scene 50. Flash of the havoc of the storm.

Scene 51. Exterior. Among the rocks, rising water. The Man meets Brother and The Girl and takes command; both dependent on him; he half supports them among the rocks.

Scene 52. Flash of the storm. (Or fearful surf.)

Scene 53. Exterior. Beneath a shelving rock. Near view. Lightning and rain. The Man, The Brother, and The Girl come underneath the shelter of the shelving rock; The Man at the edge calculating the storm's extent; The Brother and The Girl crouched behind him, The Girl clinging to his tunic and looking at him with admiration mixed with the fear in her face.

Scene 54. Flash of the storm.

Scene 54a. Repeat near view. Flash of The Man, The Girl, and The Brother as in 53.

Sub-title. THE LAST REFUGE.

Scene 55. Exterior. Rock in the water. Far view. The Man supporting the others, struggles through the water to the rock; with great difficulty, The Man puts them upon the rock and is exhausted himself. (If not too difficult, wild animals on the rocks will add to effect.)

Scene 56. Exterior. Same as 55. Near view. The Brother and The Girl on the rock, as in 55; he clings to her; she is regarding The Man in the water below.

Scene 57. Close-up of The Man in the water; exhausted and his grasp slipping.

Scene 58. Exterior. Same as 55. Near view. Group at rock, as in 55; as The Man's hold slips, The Girl reaches down to save him, and she slips from the rock.

The Man clasps her in his arms, struggling desperately to save her.

Scene 59. Close-up flash of The Brother shivering with terror alone on the rock.

Scene 60. Close-up of The Man, The Girl's arms clasped about his neck, as they sink beneath the waters. *Fade.*

END OF PROLOGUE

THE HEIR OF THE AGES

Leader. TIME UNWOUND THE SCROLL OF THE YEARS UNTIL THE EARTH BECAME GRAY AND WRINKLED, AND TO EACH LIVING THING HE LEFT A HERITAGE.

Separate Screen. THE DOG AND THE CAT TODAY TURN AROUND BEFORE LYING DOWN BECAUSE, FOR THOUSANDS OF YEARS, THE WOLF AND THE TIGER, THEIR ANCESTORS, TURNED IN EXACTLY THE SAME WAY TO PRESS DOWN THE GRASS OF THE JUNGLE INTO A COMFORTABLE BED.

Separate Screen. THE LION BORN IN CAPTIVITY IS INFURIATED BY THE SQUEAK OF A MONKEY, THOUGH HE HAS NEVER SEEN ONE. A CELL IN HIS BRAIN RECALLS THAT MONKEYS ANNOYED HIS ANCESTORS IN THE JUNGLE.

Separate Screen. MEMORY PLAYS STRANGE TRICKS. IN DREAMS, WE ALL HAVE FLASHES AND FRAGMENTS OF A DIM AND DISTANT PAST, INEXPLICABLE ON ANY GROUND SAVE THAT IT IS A HERITAGE OF THE YEARS.

Separate Screen. TYPE RECURRENCES, OR ATAVISMS, ARE FREQUENT AND UNMISTAKABLE. WHO CAN SAY THAT THEY ARE NOT IDENTITIES?

Separate Screen. HUGH PAYNE, SUPERINTENDENT OF
THE GOLCONDA MINE AT LAST CHANCE, CALIFORNIA.
Dissolve slowly into

Scene 61. Reproduce a very dim and indistinct picture
of Scene 60; hold a few feet, then, by intermingled
dissolve, there slowly comes upon the screen

Scene 62. Interior. Living room in Hugh's cabin-bun-
galow in the hills, furnished with the taste of a cul-
tured man; many books, guns, skins, trophies of the
chase, etc., and as a laboratory for testing ores; stone
fireplace and chimney; several windows; doors leading to inner rooms. Hugh bends over a specimen of
ore, examining it attentively; a roughly dressed miner
stands near, awaiting anxiously his decision.

Scene 63. Interior. Same as 62. Close-up. Hugh
slowly raises his face until he nearly faces the camera,
and looking at the miner, gravely shakes his head.
(Miner not in picture.)

Scene 64. Interior. Living room, same as 62. Hugh
and miner on, as in 62; Hugh shakes his head and
hands back the specimen; miner seems much discouraged; Hugh encourages him; calls Sing Lee, who
brings in decanter, glasses, etc.; miner drinks, Hugh
declining; miner goes; Hugh lights pipe, and resumes
a book, open on table.

Scene 64a. Exterior. Hugh's bungalow. Little better
than a shack. Hugh and miner come to door. Miner
goes. Hugh looks after him, then enters house.

Sub-Title. THE TOWN OF LAST CHANCE.

Scene 65. Street in mining town; many signs—
"Broadway and 42d St.," "The St. Regis," "Under-
taker. It Is a Pleasure to Be Buried By Me." Cut in
close-ups of these or other points of interest. Flashes.

Scene 66. Exterior. "The Square Deal"—saloon, gambling house, dance hall. Far view. Flash.

Scene 57. Exterior. "The Square Deal." Near view. Same as 66. Kearney, "Shorty," and one or two rough characters lounging near door; men, women, and girls passing and entering.

Sub-Title. KEARNEY, THE PROPRIETOR OF "THE SQUARE DEAL."

Scene 68. Close-up of Kearney's hard, evil, determined, semi-handsome face, with cigar in his mouth; face breaks into a sinister smile.

Scene 69. Exterior. Square Deal, same as 67. Near view. Group on as in 67; several of the dance hall girls come and chat with Kearney and Shorty; loud laughter and jokes; the girls turn to look at

Sub-Title. "THE DUCHESS."

Scene 70. Exterior. Square Deal, same as 66. Near view. Group on as in 69; "The Duchess" joins them leisurely and with the easy confidence of a woman who knows she is "*it.*" Her wonderfully innocent-appearing face seems out of place there; she chats with Kearney, who is not altogether indifferent to her.

Scene 71. Close-up of "The Duchess" as she talks.

Scene 72. Exterior. Square Deal. Same as 66. Near view. Group on as in 70; after a moment's chat, all turn and enter saloon, Kearney exercising undoubted proprietorship of "The Duchess."

Scene 73. Interior. The Square Deal. Large; usual equipment—bar, dance floor, roulette or faro bank, poker table, pianist and one or two other musicians; stairway leading to rooms above. Tables for drinking. Usual crowd on; Kearney, The Duchess, Shorty and girls enter and make their way to table and seat themselves; the other girls go to another table, picking up a companion or two on their way.

Scene 74.   Interior. Square Deal. Near view of Kearney's table.   Group at table as in 73; waiter (man, girl, or Chinaman) brings drinks to table; The Duchess examines her drink and is not satisfied with it; after a short parley with the waiter, she dashes glass into waiter's face; waiter retires with hands covering face; Kearney and Shorty laugh; Duchess takes Kearney's drink, swallows it, and then lights cigarette.

Scene 75.   Close-up of The Duchess's face as she smokes, rolling her eyes wickedly in the direction of the waiter.

Scene 76.   Interior. Square Deal. Near view near bar. Flash. Bartender and another waiter wipe blood from waiter's cut face.

Scene 77.   Repeat flash of 75. Duchess's face breaking into a sneering, sinister smile. Diaphragm out.

Sub-Title.   THE PROSPECTORS.

Scene 78.   Exterior. Long mountain trail. Picturesque. Flash. Hope and his daughter, Penelope, with pack mule. Far view.

Scene 79.   Near flash of group as in 78; Penelope holding mule's ear affectionately, and whispering into it.

Sub-Title.   PENELOPE AGATHA SPOTTISWOODE HOPE. TOO MUCH NAME FOR SO LITTLE A GIRL, SO FOLKS CALLED HER '' MISSY.''

Scene 80.   Close-up of Missy as she whispers into the mule's ear.

Scene 81.   Exterior. On the trail, overlooking the town. Missy, Hope, and the mule contemplate the town from eminence, then trek.

Scene 82.   Exterior. Street in Last Chance, same as 65.

Before The Square Deal. Usual crowd on; Kearney, Shorty, and The Duchess at doorway of Square Deal; the Hope outfit makes its way up the street, attracting some attention, especially from The Duchess, who points, laughing.

Scene 83. Close-up of The Duchess, as she points, laughing. Flash.

Scene 84. Exterior. Street, same as 65. Near view. Flash. The Hope outfit stops, Hope making an inquiry; Missy sees The Duchess.

Scene 85. Close-up flash of Missy as she looks indignantly at The Duchess. Cut back and forth, if thought effective.

Scene 86. Exterior. Street, same as 65. Several of the town girls gather around the Hope outfit and have fun with Missy; Hope returns and the outfit moves on, amid merriment of the girls, and the indignation of Missy.

Leader. THE HOPE FAMILY TAKES A " BUNGALOW " IN THE HILLS ABOVE THE TOWN.

Scene 87. Exterior. Rough, deserted cabin in the hills; picturesque. Hope is repairing the outside of the cabin; Missy comes from inside and admires his work; invites him in to see hers; they enter.

Scene 88. Interior. Hope's cabin; much delapidated, but made habitable by Missy's feminine touch; small bookshelf containing four books; several plates from a fashion magazine on walls; open hearth; rude table of planks and chairs same, evidently left by former occupant. Ladder to loft. Missy leads her father in, proud of her work, and points out the improvements she has made, frolicking around the pitiful rooms, happy in having a home at all; she has put wild flowers in the windows in anything that will hold them; the dinner is cooking in a pot on the hearth, and Hope sits before the fire, Missy standing by the side of it and looking into it.

Scene 89. Interior. Hope's cabin. Near view at fireplace. Group as in 88, at fire. *Fade out.*

Sub-Title. THE BOSS — NOMINAL AND ACTUAL.

Scene 90. Exterior. Offices of the mine. Rude building, near shaft. Hugh's horse tied to post; foreman comes with papers as Hugh comes from offices; foreman shows him papers and they consult.

Scene 91. Exterior. At shaft. Several men come from shaft, two of them angry and in belligerent mood toward each other; there is a disposition among the other men to take sides, and it looks like serious trouble.

Scene 92. Exterior. Same as 90. Near view. Flash. Hugh and foreman hear the noise of the controversy and go in that direction.

Scene *93.* Exterior. At shaft, same as 91. Far view. Group on, as in 91; foreman precedes Hugh into crowd but can't seem to make very great headway at stopping impending fight; Hugh strides into crowd.

Scene 94. Exterior. At shaft, same as 91. Near view. Group on as in 93; the two belligerents have drawn knives; Hugh confronts them, and they are manifestly afraid of him. He registers, "Give me those knives." The knives are handed over reluctantly; Hugh says, meaningly,

Cut-In. "I CAN'T AFFORD TO HAVE TWO MEN DISABLED, FOR I'M SHORT HANDED NOW. FURTHERMORE, I DON'T BELIEVE EITHER OF YOU IS GAME ENOUGH TO FIGHT.

BUT THE NEXT TIME YOU TWO START ANYTHING, I'LL
MAKE YOU FIGHT!"

Back to scene. Hugh turns on his heel and goes with
foreman conferring over the papers; the two men slink
away, the others laughing at them.

Scene 95. Exterior. Before offices, same as 90. Hugh
and foreman come into picture, and after a moment's
chat, Hugh unties his horse, mounts, and rides away.

Scene 96. Exterior. Hope's cabin, same as 87. Missy
stands in doorway, water-pail in hand; then, bare-
footed, bounds away.

Scene 97. Exterior. Mountain trail. Picturesque.
Flash. Hugh rides slowly, thinking.

Scene 98. Exterior. At the spring. Picturesque. Missy
bounds down to the spring; looks at her reflection in
the water.

Scene 99. Near view of Missy as she looks into water.
(Reproduce " Nature's Mirror," I believe the picture
is called.) After a moment, in which she arranges her
hair, she takes from her bosom a folded page from a
fashion magazine, such as adorn the walls of the cabin.
Cut in close-up of the extreme fashion sheet. Then back
to scene. She tries to arrange her dress in conformity
with it.

Scene 100. Exterior. Trail near the spring. Near view.
Hugh rides along trail; sees Missy, stops his horse
to watch her; looks at her in surprise, as he had no
idea of her existence before. (Here, as he looks, it is
possible that a faint, shadowy picture — scene 26 —
of The Girl as The Man saw her in the Prologue, would
be effective, conveying, of course, the dim and intang-
ible shadow of memory referred to in the titles. At
several other points in the story there is opportunity

for a similar exemplification of these memories, but they seem to me to be most difficult to " put over " in an effective way. It is a matter for consideration whether to use them at all, as the parallels are fairly plain; but I will indicate them as they occur to me. If used, diaphragm in and out and regulate Hugh's action accordingly.)

Scene 101. Exterior. At spring, same as 98. Very near view. Flash. Missy, all unconscious of Hugh's gaze, continues with her toilet.

Scene 102. Exterior. Spring, same as 98. Full view. Missy on, as in 101; Hugh rides into picture, and Missy is startled and inclined to flee precipitately, but Hugh's pleasant smile reassures her, though she hides the fashion sheet behind her, and is conscious of her bare legs; Hugh dismounts and allows his horse to drink, and talks to Missy, who though still diffident, is regaining her composure.

Scene 103. Exterior. Near view at spring, same as 98. Hugh and Missy talk, getting acquainted, though Missy keeps the fashion page hidden with an effort, and at the same time is conscious of her bare legs; Hugh introduces himself; Missy frankly offers her hand, at the same time exposing the fashion page, and says,

Cut-In. " I'M PENELOPE AGATHA SPOTTISWOODE HOPE, BUT EVERYBODY CALLS ME ' MISSY.' "

Back to scene. Hugh smiles gravely, shaking his head at the long name; they seat themselves by the spring and Hugh finally gets her to show him the fashion page, her every action betokening frank ingenuousness; he looks at the page, and has hard work to keep his face straight, but assures her that her present costume is far more fitting than the one on the page; she is pleased, but incredulous.

Scene 104. Exterior. Hope's cabin, same as 87. Flash. Hope comes to door of cabin, looks in, and finding Missy gone, calls.

Scene 105. Exterior. Spring, same as 98. Full view. Hugh and Missy on as in 103; Missy starts at the call, jumps up, and is about to say good-bye to Hugh, when he calls attention to the fact that the pail she has taken up is empty; he takes it from her and fills it, and walks with her; when they have taken a few steps, she calls his attention to the fact that he has forgotten his horse; they laugh, and Hugh gets the horse, and they go, Hugh carrying pail of water and leading horse.

Scene 106. Exterior. Hope's cabin, same as 87. Hope stands in the doorway watching them approach; Hugh, leading horse and carrying the water-pail, preceded by Missy, comes into picture; Hugh is duly presented to Hope, who sizes Hugh up, appraisingly; apparently satisfied with him, Hugh is invited into the cabin; Hugh ties his horse, and they start to enter, though Missy has some reluctance on account of appearances; she darts in ahead.

Scene 107. Interior. Hope's cabin, same as 88. Full view. Missy on, hurriedly setting things to rights — "tidying up;" Hope and Hugh enter, and there is a moment of general talk; at length Hugh notices the small shelf of books and looks at the titles; Missy at his side.

Scene 108. Interior. Hope's cabin, same as 88. Near view near books. Hugh and Missy at books, as in 107. Hugh turns to her and says,

Cut-In, " Are You Fond of Books? "

Back to scene. Missy is a little staggered, but registers " Yes." Hugh scans the titles again, endeavoring
to get her tastes, and turning to her, registers, " Which
one of these do you prefer ? " Missy ponders a moment,
then says, indicating,

Cut-In. " I THINK I PREFER THAT ONE."

Back to scene. Hugh takes out the volume indicated
and looks at the title.

Scene 109. Close-up of book; title reading, " Geodetic
Survey of Arizona," or some other equally dry and
abstruse work. Flash.

Scene 110. Interior. Same as 108 (88). Near-view.
Hugh and Missy at books, Hugh with volume in his
hand; he opens it and looks at the contents; is puzzled; shakes his head; Missy diverts the conversation
cleverly.

Scene 111. Interior. Hope's cabin, same as 88. Full
view. Hugh and Missy at the books; Hope sits near
the hearth, looking around at them and smiling
broadly; Hugh and Missy, at Missy's initiative, join
Hope at the fireside and seat themselves near him in
the glow of the fire.

Scene 112. Interior. Hope's cabin; near view of hearth.
Group on as in 111; the two men fill their pipes and
talk, Missy listening; Hugh frequently looks at Missy,
who is unconscious of his gaze, and once fails to hear
what Hope is saying, a slight confusion on Hugh's
part resulting. *Fade out.*

Leader. BACK EAST, LARRY PAYNE MAKES DUCKS AND
DRAKES OF THE LAST OF HIS FORTUNE.

Scene 112a. Interior. Larry's rooms; elegantly fitted in
bachelor style. Sitting room or den; bedroom showing beyond. Various articles of clothing distributed

about the room in disorder, and draped over the furniture picturesquely; the occupant had undressed all over the place; Larry in pajamas, is seen in the bedroom beyond, being clothed in a bath-robe by his valet, a most patient and long-suffering man; Larry enters sitting room, his hair tousled, and a manifestly bad taste in his mouth; valet hastily gathers up some of the clothes, etc., from various improper and unusual places, Larry watching him (near camera) and his face breaking into a smile in spite of his " head." Larry lights a cigarette and calls loudly for his cocktail; valet has prepared two, and Larry drinks them both, with evident relish; as valet busies himself about the room, Larry thinks. Diaphragm out on Larry's face as he thinks, and into

Scene 112b. Open diaphragm to near view of poker table, Larry and four men of fast set playing; two women in evening gowns watch the game from behind the men's chairs; one of the women bends over Larry and he indulges in little familiarities with her; Larry loses, rises from his chair and goes to lounge accompanied by the woman, and he lights a cigarette from her's, and they engage in a most animated and intimate conversation. Diaphragm out and in.

Scene 112c. Interior. Larry's rooms, same as 112a. As the vision passes, Larry smiles; valet calls his attention to a batch of letters on table; Larry runs through them hurriedly and uninterestedly, and tosses them all into wastebasket; valet says apologetically,

Cut-In. " Beg Pardon, Mr. Payne, Sir, but Several of these Creditor People Are Getting Quite Importunate, Sir; in Fact, I Might Say, Beggin' Your Pardon, Violent."

Back to scene. Larry tells him to " forget it." Valet
bows; telephone rings; valet answers, and covering
transmitter with his hand, turns inquiringly to Larry,
who waves his hand violently; valet registers, " Not
in, Sir." Evidently the person on the other end
doubts it and says something unpleasant, for valet
hangs up receiver with a shocked air; again Larry is
in reverie. Diaphragm out and in.

Scene 112d. Exterior. Road in suburbs; gay " joy ride,"
far and near views; Larry and woman in 112b prominent; pass a policeman, giving him the laugh. Diaphragm out and into

Scene 112e. Interior. Larry's rooms, same as 112a. As
vision passes, Larry smiles, and shakes his head; valet
questions him respectfully; Larry says,

Cut-In. " Never Mind, Old Top, I'll Write to Brother
Hugh if I Get Time Today, and He Will Come
Across with Enough to See Me Through Until I
Can Get that Mortgage."

Back to scene. Valet has to be satisfied; Larry lights
another cigarette; picks up the photograph of an over-
(or under-) dressed woman from the table and regards
it smilingly. *Fade out.*

Sub-Title. The Cave Man.

Scene 113. Exterior. Post Office. Street, same as 65.
Figures near camera. Night. Hugh comes from post
office with foreman; Hugh glances over many letters
and hands them to foreman, keeping one himself; foreman goes; Hugh walks along street opening letter.

Scene 114. Exterior. Square Deal. Street, same as 66.
Figures near camera. Night. Kearney and Shorty
lounge in front of saloon; Hugh comes, reading letter
by light from window.

Insert. LETTER IN MAN'S HANDWRITING.

. . . another five hundred until I can arrange about my property on 110th St. Have been going it pretty strong, but am going to pull myself together.

Yours,   LARRY.

Back to scene. Hugh stands reading the letter, frowning; Kearney and Shorty look at him; Kearney says,

Cut-In. " WHAT'S THE TROUBLE, PAYNE? BAD NEWS? COME HAVE A DRINK."

Back to scene. Hugh looks up slowly from the letter, folds it deliberately, puts it into his pocket, and walks up to Kearney, and says, grimly,

Cut-In. " MISTER PAYNE, FOR YOURS, KEARNEY. YES, VERY BAD NEWS. I'VE GOT A YOUNG BROTHER WHO IS BEING SPEEDED ON HIS WAY TO HELL BY JUST SUCH SCOUNDRELS AS YOU. I'LL GO YOU ON THAT DRINK."

Back to scene. Kearney laughs, and the three enter the saloon together.

Scene 115. Interior. Square Deal, same as 73. Night. Kearney, Hugh, and Shorty enter and make their way to the bar; on the way, several of the girls make overtures to Hugh; he regards them contemptuously, throws several pieces of money on one of the tables for them to drink up, and joins Kearney and Shorty at the bar. All show deference to Hugh, which he does not notice; all show surprise at seeing him there; whisper, etc.

Scene 116. Interior. Square Deal, same as 73. Night. Near view of bar. Hugh, Shorty, and Kearney at the bar; Kearney orders drinks which are set out; Hugh throws gold pieces on bar; Kearney remonstrates; Hugh pays no attention to him; swallows his drink and asks for more; Kearney shrugs his shoulders and lets Hugh have his way; after another drink or two have been served and drunk, Kearney speaks to Hugh, but he is morose and pays no attention to him. Cut to

Scene 117. Close-up of '' The Duchess '' as she sees Hugh.

Scene 118. Interior. Same as 116 (73). Night. Group at bar as in 116; '' The Duchess '' joins them, looking at Hugh with sneering inquisitiveness; Hugh returns her gaze unmoved; she says,

Cut-In. '' SO YOU'VE DROPPED IN TO SEE US AT LAST, MR. GOLIATH. WE THOUGHT YOU WERE A WOMAN-HATING PROHIBITIONIST.''

Back to scene. Hugh looks at her gravely and steadily, and she is uncomfortable under his gaze; he finally says, deliberately, after draining his glass, and looking over her head intently for a moment,

Cut-In. '' KEARNEY, IF THIS LADY IS A FRIEND OF YOURS, YOU WILL ADVISE HER TO WITHDRAW, AS I AM ABOUT TO START SOMETHING.''

Back to scene. Hugh starts deliberately away from the group, they following him with their eyes.

Scene 119. Interior. Square Deal, same as 73. Full view. Night. The two fighting miners (scene 94) have risen from their adjoining tables and are menacing each other, but there is really little chance of a fight; Hugh comes from the bar deliberately; they see him too late, and each tries to get away; Hugh knocks one down and hurls the other on top of him; he then hurls tables and chairs in every direction, clearing a space; the place is in an uproar, and Hugh makes havoc of the furniture; Kearney is about to interfere, but Shorty warns him that Hugh is a good man to let alone; the most interested spectator is '' The Duchess," who hovers as near as is at all safe, and watches Hugh with admiring eyes; the space cleared, Hugh stands the men up and tells them to fight; the men dare do nothing else, and Hugh watches them with the "Cave Man" look upon his face; at the least sign of quitting, Hugh menaces them, and they fight to exhaustion; (of course, with fists only) when they can no longer stand, Hugh holds them up and bids them fight; one or two of the spectators attempt to mollify Hugh, but they are thrown aside and none dares interfere. At length Hugh throws down the exhausted men contemptuously, and strides from the place. Cut in close-ups and near views of the main action — Hugh, the fighters, Kearney, and The Duchess, who is completely fascinated by The Man.

Note. The object of this scene is, of course, to show the brutal side of Hugh and his atavistic tendencies other than that of self-sacrifice; and also to prepare the way for what he does in The Square Deal afterwards. I have tried to portray Hugh as a Real Man; of strong passions and intense personality, who when deeply moved, casts aside modern conventions and restrictions, and goes back to primal " stuff." For the weak man to sacrifice and " give up," excites only pity; when the strong man does it, one feels admiration. Also, I believe the public is tired of the entirely fictional namby-pamby hero who never departs from the code prescribed by the books in a Sunday School Library. The more outrageous he is made to appear in this scene, the better it will suit my idea of the story.

Scene 120. Exterior. Square Deal, same as 65. Near view. Night. Hugh comes from the Square Deal, stands a moment, shakes himself and makes a face, as though to get the atmosphere of the place and the bad taste out of himself, and then walks away; Kearney, The Duchess, and one or two others come to the door and watch him as he goes.

Sub-Title. MIDNIGHT.

Scene 121. Interior. Hugh's living room, same as 62. Night. Hugh near camera. Hugh sits at table thinking; restless; rises and paces floor, Larry's letter in his hand; finally sits at table. (In near view.) Reads letter again. Flash of letter. Hugh lays it down and thinks; starts to write; tears it in two; writes again.

Scene 122. Hugh's hand writes, close up,

My dear Larry,

I am sending you the five hundred as you request, and am sorry to be obliged to do it, not that I regret the loss of the money, but feel that you should be able to take care of yourself. . . .

Scene 123. Interior. Hugh's living room, same as 62. Night. Hugh on, as in 121; he stops writing, tears up the letter; puts cheque into envelope without any letter, addresses and stamps it; thinks. *Fade out.*

Leader. HUGH DECIDES TO ENCOURAGE THE LITERARY TASTES OF MISSY.

Scene 124. Exterior. Hope's cabin, same as 87. Hugh rides into picture with an armful of books; knocks; Missy comes to the door, and after a moment's animated chat, in which Missy looks suspiciously at the books, they enter.

Scene 125. Interior. Hope's cabin. Same as 88. Hugh and Missy come from door, Hope on in his usual place by the hearth; he greets Hugh pleasantly, and Hugh tells the purpose of his visit and shows the books to Missy, commenting on each; Hope looks at them, grinning covertly; Missy is greatly interested and takes the books, thanking Hugh and putting them on the shelf; after a moment's talk, Hugh exit, Missy seeing him to the door and looking after him, waving; she closes the door and stands with her back against it, thinking; makes resolution; goes to shelf and selects a book; takes it with determined air to Hope and bids him read to her; he demurs strongly, but she is imperative, and Hope begins, under protest. Cut in a close-up of Missy examining the books in a panic while Hugh and Hope talk together apart.

Sub-Title. LARRY COMES TO A DECISION.

Scene 126. Interior. Larry's rooms, same as 112a. Larry is dressed for going out; valet enters with several letters; Larry scans them; takes one and throws the rest into waste basket, valet watching with worried and anxious look; Larry motions him away; valet obeys, but draws near again; Larry, near camera, opens letter and takes out cheque (which is large and plain enough to save flashing it close up); he is elated at getting it, but searches the envelope for letter; there is none; he thinks, finally turns to valet and says,

Cut-In. "HIGGINS, PACK UP. I'M GOING TO TAKE A LITTLE TRIP."

Back to scene. Higgins is astounded and enters a respectful protest — he doesn't want to be left to face all those bills — but Larry pays no attention to him, and goes leisurely; Higgins makes gesture of despair and helps himself to a drink; sits in a chair to think.

Leader. A WEEK LATER. MISSY RETURNS THE BOOKS.

Scene 127. Exterior. Trail before Hugh's bungalow.

Missy, who now has shoes and stockings and a decent dress, comes up the trail with an armful of books.

Scene 128.   Exterior.   Hugh's bungalow; same as 64a. Missy knocks on door and waits.   Knocks again.

Scene 129.   Interior.   Hugh's bedroom in bungalow; very plain.   Near view.   Flash of Hugh sleeping soundly in bed.

Scene 130.   Exterior.   Hugh's bungalow, same as 64a. Unable to get in by the door, Missy goes to window which is open and climbs into it.

Scene 131.   Interior.   Living room, same as 62.   Missy climbs into room through window, and looks about her curiously for a few moments; sees door to inner room and starts toward it.

Scene 132.   Interior.   Hugh's bedroom, same as 129. Hugh hears someone in outer room and calls '' Who is there? '' (Registers) getting half out of bed.

Scene 133.   Interior.   Living room, same as 62.   Missy on, going toward door of inner room; she pauses at door and says,

Cut-In.   '' IT'S ME.   CAN I COME IN? ''

Back to scene.   Missy starts to open door.

Scene 134.   Interior.   Hugh's bedroom, same as 129. Hugh springs from the bed and braces himself against the already opening door.

Scene 135.   Near view of Missy at door, her hand on the knob.   Flash.

Scene 136.   Near view of Hugh as he braces himself against the door and yells at her not to come in.   He is in a positive panic; then realizes the utter ingenuousness of the girl, and laughs and shouts directions through the door.

Scene 137. Interior. Living room, same as 62. Missy goes from door and seats herself demurely and looks about the room wonderingly; after a moment, Hugh enters in coat, trousers, and slippers, and greets her, opening the outer door, and realizing that she has no idea of the conventions; Missy says, indicating,

Cut-In. " I BROUGHT BACK THE BOOKS. THANK YOU SO MUCH; THEY WERE LOVELY."

Back to scene. Hugh tells her that she is very welcome, and indicating his well-filled shelves, asks if she will have some more; she hesitates; and a great light begins to break over Hugh; he takes one of the books that she has returned and handing it to her, questions her pleasantly about it; she opens the book, plainly embarrassed. Cut in a close-up of Missy with the book held upside down, and Hugh looking on and realizing that she cannot read. She looks up at Hugh and the tears begin to start; she throws the book onto the table and buries her face in her arms on the table; Hugh is plainly vexed at himself for forcing this confession from her, and pats her shoulder tenderly. Back to full view of room. Hugh and Missy on as in close-up; Hugh looks at the sobbing girl tenderly; seats himself across the table from her, and lifting up her chin, tells her that she mustn't take it so hard, and that he will be glad to teach her; she is glad at this, and after a few assurances and encouragement, she goes; Hugh closes the door after her, and stands against it thinking; then his face breaks into a smile. *Fade out.* (Possibly a cut-in by Missy admitting that she cannot read.)

Sub-Title. A LITTLE MISUNDERSTANDING.

Scene 138. Exterior. Square Deal, same as 65. Street. Kearney lounges in front of the saloon. Flash.

Scene 139. Exterior. Store on street. Same as 65. Flash. Missy comes from store with basket.

Scene 140. Exterior. Street. Same as 65. Flash. Hugh rides along street slowly reading letter.

Scene 141. Exterior. Street. Same as 65. Close up. Duchess sees Hugh and after a moment's hesitation, starts toward him.

Scene 142. Exterior. Street, same as 65. Near view. As Hugh rides slowly, reading, The Duchess comes to him in the middle of the street and he stops his horse and they talk.

Scene 143. Close-up flash of Kearney as he sees them.

Scene 144. Close-up flash of Missy as she sees them.

Scene 145. Exterior. Street, same as 65. Near view. Duchess talks to Hugh coquettishly, urging; says,

Cut-In. " WHY DON'T YOU DROP IN TO SEE US AGAIN? THERE HAS BEEN NO EXCITEMENT SINCE YOU SPENT THE EVENING THERE."

Back to scene. Hugh laughs and says that he thinks one call was enough; The Duchess urges using all her arts, knowing that Kearney is looking.

Scene 146. Close-up flash of Kearney, angry and jealous.

Scene 147. Close-up flash of Missy, surprised and a little jealous, but evidently trying to dismiss it from her mind.

Scene 148. Same as 145 (65).

Hugh laughingly declines The Duchess's invitation; she is most flirtatious, and from a distance, the meeting would seem to be a most happy one; at last, she

leaves him with a coquettish courtsey, and Hugh rides
away, laughing.

Scene 149. Exterior. Square Deal. Same as 66. Figures near camera. Kearney at door in ill humor;
The Duchess comes airily; tantalizes him; he plainly
remonstrates with her; she looks at him steadily,
smiling; says,

Cut-In. " WHY DON'T YOU SPEAK TO MR. PAYNE
ABOUT IT? I CAN'T HELP IT IF THE MEN LIKE ME! "
Back to scene. Kearney is angrier than ever; The
Duchess laughs at him tantalizingly, and enters the
saloon; Kearney thinks; Hope comes into picture and
tries to enter the saloon, but Missy is on his trail and
grabs his coat-tail; lectures him roundly, and he is
most submissive; goes with her like a lamb, though
it is plain that he has been drinking; Kearney looks
after them malevolently; turns and enters saloon.
Cut in close-ups if thought effective.

Sub-Title. AS THE WEEKS PASS, THE INTIMACY RIPENS,
AND UNDER THE INSPIRATION OF HER LOVE FOR HUGH,
MISSY MAKES RAPID PROGRESS.

Scene 150. Exterior. Hope's cabin, same as 87. (Or
picturesque spot.) Missy reads to Hugh from book,
Hugh correcting her mistakes; she is manifestly bright
and anxious to learn, and it is plain she is doing well;
Hope comes, and it is plain that he has been drinking
heavily; he is extravagantly polite to Hugh, but
stumbles going in the door; Missy is greatly embarrassed; she says, in answer to Hugh's look of inquiry
as to whether she needs any help,

Cut-In. " NO, I DON'T RECKON I NEED ANY HELP.
HE'S ALWAYS GENTLE, AND MINDS ME, BUT I CAN'T
WATCH HIM ALL THE TIME. WHEN HE GETS GOOD

AND PICKLED, HE QUITS. HE'LL BE GOOD FOR QUITE
A WHILE, FOR HE'S SURE PLASTERED NOW."
Back to scene. Hugh laughs at her quaint way of
expression, and after a few instructions in regard to
lessons, he goes; Missy sits with her chin in her hands,
looking atfer him.

Sub-Title. LESSONS.— FOR BOTH.

Scene 151. Interior. Hope's cabin, same as 88. Night.
Firelight. Near view. Missy works feverishly on
her lessons, appealing now and then for help to her
father, who sits, nodding, in his place by the hearth;
cut in close-ups of each. Back to scene. Hope tries
to sleep, but Missy keeps him stirred up asking for
assistance, and he is meek about it.

Scene 152. Interior. Hope's cabin, same as 88. Night.
Firelight. Full view. Missy finishes with her lessons; she lights her candle at the fire; and after
bidding her father goodnight, she mounts the ladder
to her loft above; Hope makes a great show of taking
off his coat and boots and preparing for bed; sits on
the side of his bunk; thinks; diaphragm out and in
— vision of the Square Deal in full blast. Diaphragm
out. Hope looks at the top of the ladder tentatively;
no sound; resolves to take a chance.

Scene 153. Close-up or very near view, of Missy at
aperture in floor of loft near top of ladder waiting;
in night clothes.

Scene 154. Interior. Hope's cabin, same as 88. Night.
Firelight. Full view. Hope hurriedly dons his coat
and with his boots in his hand, starts for the door on
tip-toe; Missy comes down the ladder part way; he
halts, and they look at each other; cut in close-up of
each. Back to scene. Hope weakens, returns duti-

fully, takes off his coat, and Missy goes up the ladder; not a word spoken; no ill feeling; Hope starts to undress, resignedly.

Sub-Title. LAST CHANCE GETS A WELCOME INCREASE IN ITS POPULATION.

Scene 155. Exterior. Square Deal. Street, same as 65. Stage (or buckboard which Larry has hired) drives into street, and Larry alights; impresses a bystander into service, who carries his two big grips, and makes straight for the Square Deal, followed by the grips and man. They enter.

Scene 156. Interior. Square Deal, same as 73. Larry enters, followed by man with grips; usual crowd on; Larry goes at once to the bar, and in a few moments, is well acquainted with Kearney, Shorty, and several of the girls; he buys liberally; The Duchess joins the party and at once, Larry has eyes for no one but her; Kearney does not mind it, as it is the usual process of " milking a sucker," at which The Duchess is an adept; Larry is at once popular, especially after he makes known his identity; and after quite a jolly party, he is directed aright and sets out, shaking hands with most everybody. Cut scene with close-ups and near views — especially of Larry and The Duchess, who has taken a decided fancy to him; after he is gone, they agree that he is all right.

Scene 157. Interior. Hugh's living room, same as 62. Hugh busy with a mass of papers; the door opens, and Larry steps into room, throwing in his grips ahead of him; the two brothers look at each other for a moment, and then, with genuine joy, rush into each other's arms and clasp hands heartily; then they seat themselves for a talk; after a moment, Larry says, frankly, (After they seat themselves, in Near View.)

Cut-In. " OLD MAN, I'VE COME OUT HERE TO MAKE A MAN OF MYSELF. I NEVER COULD GET AWAY FROM THAT JOY STUFF AS LONG AS I STAYED IN NEW YORK. I'M GOING TO START ALL OVER. CAN YOU GET ME A JOB? "

Back to scene. Hugh looks at him and his frankness carries conviction; Hugh reaches out his hand and shakes his brother's heartily; Larry indicates that he could use a drink; Hugh hesitates a moment, then calls the Chinaman, who brings in decanter and glasses; Larry pours out a stiff drink; Hugh declines; Larry drains his glass and talks happily. *Fade out.*

Sub-Title. NEXT MORNING.

Scene 158. Interior. Living room, same as 62. Hugh and Larry at breakfast, served by the Chinaman; Hugh finishes and says that he must get to the mine early; tells Larry to take possession, and goes. Larry idles over his breakfast, smokes a cigarette, and " kids " the Chinaman as he clears away the things (Lapse of time enough to let Hugh get away from the house). As Larry sits contemplating things, and in most cheerful frame of mind, the door opens, and Missy, with several books, enters; they confront each other in surprise, Larry being delighted. " All the comforts of a home! Hugh certainly has a nice place! " (Cut-in ?) Larry rising, offers Missy a chair, which she takes as though hypnotized, and in a minute Larry's fluency has swept her off her balance, and she is listening to him entranced; she finally gets a chance to tell him who she is and that she has brought back the books; Larry insists that she take some more, and that he will carry them home for her;

she has no chance to object, as Larry is a fast worker;
and she declining an invitation from him "to stay
and visit a while, and have a little breakfast, or a
drink," he loads himself up with books, tucks her
under his arm, and they go, Missy half bewildered,
but pleased, nevertheless. Cut in close-ups and near
views as effective.

Scene 159. Exterior. On the trail from the bungalow,
same as 127. Flash Larry and Missy go down the
trail in animated conversation.

Scene 160. Exterior. Before the shaft, same as 91.
Flash. Hugh hard at work, checking up men (or
some other detail of mining).

Scene 161. Exterior. Hope's cabin, same as 87.
Larry, perfectly at home, seated explaining to the
entranced Missy all about New York and the tall
buildings. Diaphragm out.

Leader. CALLED AWAY FOR A MONTH TO THE MAIN
OFFICE OF THE MINE IN SAN FRANCISCO, HUGH LEAVES
LARRY IN POSSESSION.

Scene 162. Exterior. Railroad station in West. Platform. Hugh bids Larry and the foreman goodbye as
train pulls in, boards train, as it pulls out.

Scene 163. Train recedes down long stretch of track;
diaphragm down on train as it disappears in the
distance.

Sub-Title. EVENINGS.

Scene 164. Interior. Hope's cabin, same as 88. Night.
Missy, Larry, and Hope, who occasionally nods in his
chair, but wakes unexpectedly, and joins in the conversation. Larry most entertaining; finally looks at
his watch and goes, accompanied to door by Missy.

Scene 165. Exterior. Hope's cabin, same as 87.

Night. Moonlight on faces. In near view, Larry and Missy step from the cabin and Larry extols the beauty of the night; talks well and earnestly to Missy, who seems to be under a spell when in his presence; Larry, perhaps, does not make love to her directly, but he has a way of impressing her and makes the most of it; finally says goodbye, and holds her hand, unresisting, just a trifle too long; then goes, with a sigh and a manly walk; Missy looks after him, puzzled at herself; looks at her hand; then suddenly enters cabin and slams door.

Scene 166. Interior. Hope's cabin, same as 88. Missy near camera. Night. Missy stands with her back against door thinking; Hope nods in his chair. Fade in a vision of Hugh's face. Then back to scene. As the vision passes, Missy comes to herself; lights the candle at the fire, and goes slowly up the ladder.

Scene 167. Interior. Square Deal, same as 73. Night. Place in full blast; usual crowd; Larry enters and is at once the center of attraction; buys a drink for several of the men; buys one for several of the girls; takes seat at the roulette table, and The Duchess hangs over his chair; Kearney pulls her away and whispers to her angrily; she flouts him and returns to back of Larry's chair; he makes a bet for her and she collects it, and rewards him with a kiss; all of which does not tend to put Kearney in a better frame of mind; but Larry is too good a " client " to be offended, and the game goes on. Fast action, cut in close-ups and near views of Larry and The Duchess, Duchess and Kearney; and of the kiss, which Kearney sees. Larry loses in the end at the roulette or faro table.

Sub-Title. IN SAN FRANCISCO.

Scene 168. Interior. Any large room. Hugh speaks to the Board of Directors of the mine, and brings them to his way of thinking; they acknowledge that he is right; shake hands with him as they pass out; Hugh left alone, gathers up his papers and stands thinking; smiles. Fade in a vision of Missy. As vision fade out, Hugh smiles again, happily, puts on his hat and goes. When left alone, Hugh in close-up or near-view. Then back to full scene.

Leader. AND THEN . . .

Scene 169. Exterior. Picturesque spot in woods. (Or any other better location.) Missy and Larry; he is talking to her earnestly; her attitude is that of surprise, yet not of anger; Larry attempts to take her hand; she draws away; he has never acted like this before; finally Larry says,

Cut-In. " MISSY, WILL YOU MARRY ME? "

Back to scene. Missy looks at him in startled surprise, smiling nervously; he advances toward her, and she darts away, looking back and smiling; he starts to pursue, but sees that it is useless; stands; Missy runs out of the picture, still looking back and smiling; Larry stands thinking; he mistakes the attitude of the girl for bashful maidenhood; he stands; thinks, smiles. *Fade out.* (The point is, that she did not say " No." This gives a basis for what he says to Hugh in a later scene.)

Sub-Title. THE HOME COMING.

Scene 170. Interior. Hugh's living room, same as 62. Night. Larry on, just finishing dinner, served by the Chinaman; Hugh comes happily, and the brothers greet each other cordially; Hugh seats himself and tells the Chinaman to bring him everything in the

house as he is ravenous; Chinaman grins and retires;
Hugh talks animatedly for a moment, Larry being a
little abstracted; finally Larry says, toying with his
spoon,

Cut-In. " OLD MAN, I HAVE SOME NEWS TO TELL YOU,
THAT I'M SURE YOU'LL BE GLAD TO HEAR. YOU
OFTEN SAID THAT THE BEST THING I COULD DO WAS
TO MARRY — IT WOULD STEADY ME. I'M GOING TO
TAKE YOUR ADVICE. I'M GOING TO MARRY THAT
LITTLE MISSY HOPE."

Back to scene. Hugh looks at his brother.

Scene 171. Close-up of Hugh as he looks, his face
changing from surprised shock, and gradually harden-
ing, the passions boiling underneath an almost perfect
control (Possibly a shadowy cut-back to the scene in
the cave. Then back to close-up); Hugh glares at
Larry, and says,

Cut-In. " HAVE YOU ASKED HER? "

Back to scene. Hugh glares at Larry.

Scene 172. Interior. Living room, same as 62. Near
view of table. Larry and Hugh on as in 170; Hugh
awaits the answer intently; Larry laughs, and says,

Cut-In. " YES — AND SHE DID NOT SAY ' NO.' I AM
SURE SHE LOVES ME."

Back to scene. Larry says cut-in and reaches out his
hand, registering " Congratulate me! " Hugh looks
into his brother's face, the instincts of the Cave Man
struggling for expression; for a moment, it is a toss-up
whether Hugh is going to murder or congratulate
him.   (Fade in a dim picture of that scene in the
prologue where The Man looks at His Brother and
The Girl in the cave, when he first is aware that The
Girl prefers His Brother.)   Then back to scene.

Slowly the old instinct of self-sacrifice for his brother wins the mastery, and Hugh reaches out and grasps his brother's hand; the Chinaman places Hugh's dinner before him, but he does not see it; the volatile Larry, wrapped up in himself, has not seen the tremendous volcano of passion that is boiling beneath Hugh's iron exterior, jumps up, lights a cigarette, selects a couple of books, puts on his cap, and with a cheery, " So long! I'm off to see her now," goes. Hugh thinks, looking straight ahead.

Scene 173. Close-up, or very near view of Hugh as he thinks; he is toying with a very heavy silver fork; in a moment, the fork is wound and twisted in his fingers, though he is not aware of it. *Fade out.* (Possibly, the effect of this will be heightened by cutting in a very close-up *flash* of his powerful hands twisting the fork).

Sub-Title. CONFIRMATION.

Scene 174. Exterior. In the mountains (or woods). Night. Hugh walks aimlessly, keeping down the passion that threatens to rise.

Scene 175. Exterior. Trail near Hope's cabin; cabin in distance; light from inside. Hugh near camera. Night. Hugh comes into picture and stops, looking; in the distance, near the open cabin door, Larry and Missy come (In silhouette) (?). She talks to Larry earnestly, looking up into his face, her hands in his; Hugh sees this.

Scene 176. Exterior. Hope's cabin, same as 88. Night. Light from fire. Hope in chair; looks about him, sees Missy not there; goes to door and looks out; coast clear; puts on hat and coat and hurries out stealthily.

Scene 177. Exterior. Trail near Hope's cabin, same

as 175. Night. Near view. Light from open door.
Night. Larry and Missy on as in 175; he holds her
hands and she looks up into his face and says,

Cut-In. " No, LARRY, I DON'T LOVE YOU THAT WAY.
DON'T ASK ME AGAIN. I CAN'T TELL YOU ANY
MORE — PLEASE."

Back to scene. Larry pleads, still holding her hands,
and she gently tells him " No."

Scene 178. Exterior. Near cabin. Night. Hugh, near
camera, Larry and Missy, in distance, as in 175 and
177; Hugh, of course, cannot hear what is said; his
face hardens and he turns away in agony.

Scene 179. Exterior. Trail near Hope's cabin, near
view. Night. Light from open door. Same as 175.
After a moment of unavailing pleading, in which
Larry attempts to take her into his arms and she
gently repulses him, Larry goes; Missy stands looking
after him in pity, then turns and enters.

Scene 180. Interior. Hope's cabin, same as 88. Night.
Light from fire. Missy enters; and almost at once
notices that her father is gone; fade in, if there is
any doubt of her intention " getting over," a short
vision of the bar of the Square Deal, with Hope there
drunk. Then back to scene. Missy assures herself
that he has taken his hat, and then, thinking a
moment, goes, with determination.

Scene 181. Flash of Larry hurrying down the trail
toward town. Night.

Scene 182. Near view flash of Hugh as he sees him;
thinks; follows, worried. Night.

Scene 183. Street in town. Exterior, same as 65.
Night. Larry passes along street rapidly; Hugh lurks
some distance behind watching.

Scene 184. Flash of Missy going down the trail, same as 181. Night.

Scene 185. Interior. The Duchess' room above The Square Deal; rough room, but tawdrily furnished. Night. Duchess near camera. The Duchess preens herself for the evening.

Scene 186. Interior. Square Deal, same as 73. Night. Few people. Larry enters and looks about; Kearney is not there; he inquires at table of girls for The Duchess; they smile and indicate that she is upstairs; Larry hesitates a moment, then goes up the stairs; girls smile and whisper.

Scene 187. Interior. Rude hall, lighted by kerosene lamp. Night. Larry comes along hall, opens a door as though he had been there before and enters.

Scene 188. Interior. The Duchess's room, same as 185. Night. The Duchess on, as in 185; Larry enters, and she greets him cordially; he throws down his hat and sits near her. *Cut to*

Scene 189. Interior. Square Deal, same as 73. Night. People on, as in 186; Hugh enters and looks about; Larry not there; he goes to bar and orders drink; man at bar whispers to him that Larry is upstairs; Hugh turns from his drink, thinks a moment, then mounts stairs.

Scene 190. Exterior. Square Deal, same as 66. Night. Flash. Missy comes; hesitates.

Scene 191. Interior. Hall, same as 187. Flash. Night. Hugh comes along hall and hesitates before doors.

Scene 192. Interior. Square Deal, same as 73. Night. People on, as in 186; Missy enters timidly and looks around for her father; he is not there; the girls see her and surround her.

Scene 193. Interior. Square Deal, same as 73. Night. Near view of group as in 192. After a moment's banter, one of the girls says,

Cut-In. " WHY DON'T YOU GO UPSTAIRS AND SEE YOUR FRIEND, HUGH PAYNE? HE'S CALLING ON THE DUCHESS ! "

Back to scene. Missy says it's a lie, her spunk rising; they show her to the stairs and dare her to go up; Missy hesitates, but goes pluckily.

Scene 194. Interior. Duchess's room, same as 185. Night. Larry and Duchess on, in rather familiar attitude; door opens and Hugh appears; he stands a moment, looking at them in contempt, then crosses room, so that he faces the door; he says nothing, only looks; Larry quails and starts a stammering defense or excuse; Missy appears in the doorway, and Hugh alone sees her, she being back of Larry and The Duchess; Missy steps nearer; Hugh's face changes; he is going to " cover " for Larry; Hugh puts his arm about The Duchess and says,

Cut-In. " No, LARRY, I WON'T GO HOME WITH YOU. YOU HAVE NO RIGHT TO INTERFERE WITH ME. I'M GOING TO STAY HERE. THIS IS MY GIRL."

Back to scene. Missy comes into the room looking only at Hugh; Larry realizes what Hugh is doing, and not having given up hope of getting Missy, he allows the sacrifice; after a long look at Hugh, Missy covers her face with her hands and runs from the room; at a sign from Hugh, Larry slinks after her, leaving The Duchess nestling in Hugh's bosom; once they are gone, Hugh throws her from him roughly; she pleads with him to take her; Hugh looks at her in contempt; Kearney bursts in with drawn gun;

Hugh looks at him calmly; Kearney rages, and Hugh is not affected in any way; finally the disquieting calmness of Hugh gets on Kearney's nerves, and he is plainly not going to shoot; Hugh says, calmly,

Cut-In. " KEARNEY, IF YOU SHOULD SHOOT ME WITH THAT THING AND I FOUND OUT ABOUT IT, I MIGHT DO YOU SOME HARM. I'M GOING NOW. YOU DIDN'T THINK I WANTED THAT — CARRION, DID YOU? "

Hugh says cut-in, indicating The Duchess; he takes his hat and stalks from the room, turning his back upon them; The Duchess crumples in a heap on the floor, and Kearney looks at her. Duchess sneers at him; this infuriates him and, gun in hand he rushes out of the door. Duchess alarmed. (Cut scene with close-ups of main action — Hugh in door; Missy as she sees Hugh; Larry; and of Hugh and Kearney, as Kearney's nerve leaves him.)

Scene 195. Interior. Square Deal, same as 73. Night. Crowd on; Larry and Missy; Hugh comes down the stairs, and starts across room to door; Kearney comes part way down the stairs and fires at Hugh; great confusion; Hugh turns and rushes for the stairs and up them, Kearney backing and shooting; but Hugh does not stop. Place in an uproar; Larry talking to Missy earnestly, and there is no doubt as to what he is saying, for Missy is frantic, and wants to run to Hugh's assistance, but Larry holds her.

Scene 196. Interior. Hall, same as 187. Flash. Night. Kearney backs along hall, Hugh after him; Kearney shoots, and backs into Duchess's room, Hugh after him.

Scene 197. Interior. Duchess' room, same as 185. Kearney runs in and Hugh follows, The Duchess runs toward Hugh evidently to protect him, and as Kearney shoots, she falls; Hugh turns to look at her, and Kearney shoots again (Not more than four shots should be fired by Kearney altogether); again Hugh turns upon Kearney, and The Duchess, half-rising, takes a lamp from the table, and throws it at Kearney, and the room is in flames; there is a flash of a shot, semi-darkness and smoke, during the time it takes Hugh to kill Kearney with his hands. (Or, better, perhaps, silhouetted near-view of Hugh strangling Kearney.) Flames and smoke fill the room.

Scene 198. Interior. Square Deal, same as 73. Great excitement; smoke pouring down from above and a panic is under way.

Scene 198a. Flash of Duchess' room by light of fire, showing Duchess dead. Hugh starts to drag her out, but sees she is dead, and is driven off by flames.

Scene 199. Interior. Square Deal, same as 73. Night. Near view. Much smoke. Missy and Larry talking; she says,

Cut-In. "HE CAME HERE TO SAVE YOU! WHY DON'T YOU SAVE HIM — OR LET ME?"

Back to scene. Missy tries to get to Hugh but is blocked.

Scene 200. Interior. Hall, same as 187. Flash. Night. Hugh comes from the room and through the thick smoke in the hall.

Scene 201. Interior. Square Deal, same as 73. Night. Principals near camera. Flash of the panic; Larry knocked down and under a table; Missy hemmed in. Much smoke.

Scene 201. Flash of the exterior, same as 66. Much smoke. Night.

Scene 202. Interior. Square Deal, same as 73. Night. Near view. Hugh fights his way out of the door.

Scene 203. Interior. Near view. Another part of room (73). Near view of Larry unconscious under table; Missy hemmed in. Much smoke. Flash.

Scene 204. Exterior. Same as 65. Near view of door. Much smoke. Night. Hugh near door, helping drag people out; Old Man Hope comes to Hugh, gesticulating wildly, and telling him that Missy and Larry are in there yet; as soon as Hugh " gets " this, he fights his way back into the saloon.

Scene 205. Interior. Square Deal, same as 73. Thick smoke. Near view. Night. Hugh gropes his way to Larry and Missy; a burning beam has fallen across the table, and Hugh tears that and the table away; picks up both Larry and Missy and staggers away through the smoke; as he gathers them into his arms, fade in a shadowy yet unmistakable picture of The Man, The Brother, and The Girl at the rock in the deluge, scene 55. Then back to scene. Hugh staggers away with his burden.

Scene 206. Exterior. Same as 65. Much smoke. Near view. Night. Hugh staggers from the door and toward the street, with Larry and Missy in his arms. Flash.

Scene 207. Exterior. Street, same as 65. Crowd on. Night. Hugh staggers into the crowd, and rejecting all offers of assistance, he lays them gently on the ground; Larry is dead; Missy semi-conscious. (Appropriate positions at time of taking.) Hugh's grief over the dead Larry, he finally stands, his face upturned; Missy crawls to his feet, and clings to his hand; he bends down and lifts her to his breast, looks into her eyes and realizes that she is safe; then looks at the dead Larry; then raises his face to Heaven, with Missy clasped close to his breast. Diaphragm out on their two faces. Latter part of scene shows only the three people.